LETTERS
OF A CANADIAN
STRETCHER
BEARER

ISBN: 978-1-6673-0531-8 paperback
ISBN: 978-1-6673-0532-5 hardcover

LETTERS OF A CANADIAN STRETCHER BEARER

BY

R. A. L

EDITED BY

ANNA CHAPIN RAY

BOSTON
LITTLE, BROWN AND COMPANY
1918

𝕹𝖔𝖗𝖜𝖔𝖔𝖉 𝕻𝖗𝖊𝖘𝖘
Set up and electrotyped by J. S. Cushing Co., Norwood, Mass., U.S.A.
Presswork by S. J. Parkhill & Co., Boston, Mass., U.S.A.

EDITOR'S NOTE

For military reasons, it has been judged wiser to withhold the full name of the Canadian Stretcher Bearer until the close of the war.

However, it may interest his readers to know that he is an Old Country-man, although he is now in the Canadian Expeditionary Force, and earlier had lived in the States. On the 31st May, 1915, he enlisted. Six weeks later, with the earliest of our letters, we find him in England, and rebelling against the unsatisfactory nature of service in what he caustically terms a Safety-First battalion. It was only a matter of time, however, before he caused himself to be transferred to hospital service, crossing to France to take a place as orderly in No. 3 Canadian General Hospital at Boulogne, where he arrived early in 1916. From that time on until the 23rd August, 1917, when he was gassed and sent to Blighty, the story has been left entirely in his own hands, to tell it as convincingly as may be.

Since then, he has been, first in hospital in England, then in the First Reserve Battalion, awaiting the call back to service in the trenches.

This call, however, is sounding fainter and more remote. A cable has been received, this morning, saying that he is being sent back to Canada, his active service at an end.

OTTAWA,
Fifth December,
Nineteen Seventeen.

CONTENTS

I
BLIGHTY

LETTERS OF A CANADIAN STRETCHER BEARER

I

BLIGHTY

Shorncliffe, Kent, England,
July, 1915.

Lai dearest,—

I want to keep writing letters that will give you real impressions. I mean impressions that will convey the exact condition over here, because conditions here are not even faintly similar to anything you and I have seen together. It is difficult however,—not only getting the exact impressions, but getting them down on paper. I am writing this on a doubtful table laden with cheap "pots" (pardon, *dishes*), surrounded by a very hungry crowd waiting for the dinner call. Writing is hard, but I'll do my best.

To go 'way back. We only learned recently how near we came to being torpedoed. It was very near—about a mile, to be exact. I remember seeing a lighthouse one morning and

3

then in a few hours another one — yet it was the same. I thought at the time it was funny; now I know we had turned right around, and beat it back some distance. Then another destroyer came up, also—luckily, I guess—a dense fog. Anyhow we're here. It was kind of exciting, though.

We are in huts: our work is merely fatigue work of no interest. It isn't that I want to tell you; hut of the things I have learned about this greatest of world upheavals. . . .

Well, — dinner is over, in a rush, like a lot of wild animals — beef, potatoes, rice pudding — the same always. And now I am writing on my bed, an affair of boards six inches from the ground and rather low.

I don't know how to begin to tell you "things" ; but my main impression is that I should have been here long ago, — also, not in a "safety first" corps. This thing is so terrific, this war, that a Canadian in Canada cannot possibly grasp it.

You cannot imagine men arriving here in this camp, getting an order at six p.m. to be at the station at seven — no sleep that night — running like hell — cross the Channel and next go right into a trench. And do you know that they have gone back into armour again in this war— that the thing is so desperately fierce that a rifle is becoming of no use, only high explosive shells, then knives and hand grenades? Men come back, recovered from wounds, for three days' leave; and have to go right back to it again—back to face it all. And all the men—every one—agree that it is indescribable. You must never expect to come back. As long as the sun shines, we shall never drive them—the Germans—out of Belgium. We shall win; but not that way.

Also all agree that the Huns (and you soon get the habit of using that word) do not play the game. They have ten machine guns to our one, as close as twenty-five yards apart—when our men have in cases been given orders to fire as little as six shells only at a time. But the Germans cannot stand—will not stand. This is not just rumour; but what I've gathered from dozens of talks to dozens of men. The great difficulty is to distinguish between rumour and fact. But I am being careful to tell you what I am sure of.

The atrocities are facts.

And here is an extraordinary fact: the Saxons will not fight against us, and they have to be split up here and there with Prussian regiments. . . .

The things that really matter are not in any papers. Hull has been raided more than once. On one occasion over one hundred were killed. Three times last week, Zeppelins tried to locate this camp and failed. It was read out in Orders. Aeroplanes scout round, night as well as day, and in the Channel just over the cliff lie sometimes destroyers—sometimes cruisers.

This letter is bound to be disconnected; but you must piece it together.

Wounded do not have to wear belts or puttees; others do. That is one way of telling. Another is to look in their faces. I can tell one at a glance; I can even tell you the man who has been over, without asking. That's what you call it—"being over." . . . It doesn't sound much but—it means a lot.

I cannot tell you about London, all at once. First, though, it is the only town. Once again I am sure of it.

But what a London now!

London, the stiff, stuck-up place, doesn't resemble itself in the least. There are just as many Belgium—French—soldiers on the street as English, little boys of about fourteen; French is spoken almost as much as English, and everywhere are wounded—in blue hospital suits, in carriages and pairs, in autos, and on top of 'buses in parties. I was there for two nights and two days. I was alone, but they won't let you be alone—at least that was my experience. They want to talk to you. Once the town, as I remember it, only just woke up about ten p.m. Now all is quiet soon after ten.

The entrance to Hyde Park looked quaint with a huge searchlight on top painted a dark grey, and beside it, in a kind of shed, what I took to be an anti-aircraft gun.

15 July, '15.

It is all too vast to comprehend, as one has nothing to compare it with. . . . On Sunday I saw several aeroplanes rise out of the hills at the back of here, and wing their way over to France. Only a few years ago, Lord Northcliffe paid fifty thousand dollars to the first man to fly over, and the fact was a world sensation. At H——there are a fleet of automobiles that at a distance look just like ordinary grey machines till you get close. Then you see each is mounted with a high-angle gun. It all seems so out of place in these little quiet English lanes, all drowsing in the hot summer sun. The brambles are growing on the hedges just the same. The sheep dot the little green fields, and old women bustle around their little rose-covered cottages, everything just like it always is, — when all of a sudden a line of huge grey trucks goes tearing through the narrow lane, stirring up great clouds of dust, each machine with Canada painted on its grey side and a couple of Canucks, who have no notion what " speed limit" means, on the front seat. Inside may be anything from bread to guns. The natives don't even look up from their work. No one even glances at marching men, or aeroplanes, or anything. All this is quite natural now. Suddenly you round a turn, and come on long, long, long lines of sweating, marching men in full kit, rifle, and everything—band in front. They are on a route march. Tremendous things they are, too, as two men who fell out and died last week could no doubt have testified, if they had lived. Sometimes these are undertaken at nights—unexpectedly. Near our camp are men without puttees, and with walking sticks. They are wounded convalescent. And away over on the other side are the big hospitals where the wounded are cared for. I don't know how many there are of those; but one of our men who has been attached to the Medical Corps does nothing all day long but carry men on a stretcher from the operating tables to the long lines of ambulance cars which whizz them away to their particular quarters. He says the number is staggering. And all this is only in one wee corner of this affair.

There is nothing I suppose for me to tell you about the war. You know all the news at the same time as I do, and it's less confusing. As I write, a man is sitting in the hut, a P.P.C.L.I., wounded in the legs. You may notice I mention the Patricia's a lot. It's because we are quartered next to them and so see a lot of them. Also, I still think they are the best outfit here.

The big trouble I have in describing things to you is that I have only hearsay to go by, and so far have only been able to talk to "single-idea men", those who only talk of that which they themselves have done and seen, therefore narrow. It's impossible to get a general idea. However I guess if I were there myself, I would be the same. I couldn't get a broad idea, only seeing a limited view. One thing however is very, very certain—the trenches are Hell. No other word comes anywhere near describing it. One thing may help you to form an idea of the feeling in the trenches; the men play cards a lot, but they don't take any trouble to finesse or play carefully. They bet all the money they have. When they are on leave, they spend all their money. Of what use, they say, is money to you ? Of what use to think of the future ? There isn't going to be one.

Another thing: it would be very hard for you, I know, to realize that the Canadians are only
        a very tiny, tiny drop in all this ocean of ^
(Can't find word.) What I mean is—you only hear of the Canucks, and England is intensely proud of them; but—they are nothing by comparison. My county, Yorkshire, has fifteen battalions of volunteers in France now—all volunteers at twenty-five cents a day.

What do you think of my going to the front." Perhaps to get promotion and really do something? I am slightly indifferent—that is, just at the moment. At other times, mostly when talking to men just come back or just going over, I want to be in it. But—also I want to be with you and Bill [1] again. You'd better hurry and say "go" or "stay." Which? I'd sooner go under altogether than come back wounded. *I've never yet seen a wounded man that looked as though he'd ever he good for anything any more.* And that is a big thing to say, but it's true. I hope I'm wrong.

Two weeks ago, we turned out hatless in the pouring rain to cheer a draft of Princess Pats on their way to the boat. Yesterday we heard they had been slashed to pieces, and now another draft must go.

It rains here every day—every day without fail. Some say it's the bombardment over the Channel. I don't know. Certainly—though I haven't much to say for the English climate at any time—this surely is the limit. And cold ! I freeze nearly every night with three blankets, and often have to get my overcoat on the bed to keep warm.

17 August, '15.

Just had dinner, got my transfer signed by the doctor this morning. Think I must have been passed before I was examined, as he only just glanced at me without getting out of his chair, and said I was passed. The next I hear will be my name in Orders as transferred from the —— to the C.A.M.C. Thank God! Guess

[1] The writer's daughter.

I'll be a little more useful than ornamental from now on, and can take a larger part in this war; and if I get back, will at least have a feeling that I attempted something, however little. A C.A. M.C. draft is going over very soon. I hope I get in it and can start to be of use at once.

Yesterday all the Canadians were reviewed by the Princess Alexandra of Teck. As usual, it poured with rain — it's raining as I write this — It rains every day — There is a rumour the King inspects us this week sometime.

Reviews are a nuisance to the men. They all hate them.

18 August, '15.

Last night a number of destroyers in the Channel began "talking" in their peculiar sharp yapping way with their sirens, just for all the world like a bunch of fox terriers on the scent of a rabbit. Then guns began to speak. It only lasted a few minutes. I suppose it was an airship again, or maybe just a false alarm; nothing very serious, anyhow, but a little exciting — particularly to those who have no experience at gun fire.

A man just returned from London says that when immediate orders for the return of certain units to their regiments are given out, the news is flashed on the cinema screens, and any men there beat it to the nearest station.

There are no orders respecting my transfer yet. It has gone through, of course; but it has to be on the Daily Orders before I move over. Wish it would come. This is monotonous and I may miss the next draft. If I do, the wait may be interminable. That's one of the main hardships in the army — at least on active service — the uncertainty and the long, long waits. I have heard that some men go crazy in the trenches when the order is delayed for some reason, after being given for a charge. And in a minor way the long wait for reviews, on special parades, and the uncertainty of moves are all irritating to the last degree. I can't even begin to imagine why a man should want to be a soldier in peace time.

(Noon) 19 August, '15.

Still no orders about the transfers. Worked up at clinic. More patients by about a dozen than we could possibly attend to. Very lovely morning. Got further details about the Zepp. raid of last night. All reports forget to state that a fleet of Zeppelins reached London and made a regular killing. Bad news has been suppressed, but men are coming in all the time today who went yesterday up to see the damage done. It was pretty bad, whole streets being torn up.

Why the deuce they fail to find this camp, beats me altogether. There are today fifty thousand men — soldiers — camped in a few square miles here, yet all the silly fools can do is to drop bombs on towns and kill civilians. I won't believe they don't know, almost to a man, just how many are here and where we are. Yet they never come. . . .

20 August, '15.

I wonder if President Wilson will send a note or only just a picture postcard over this latest atrocity. What on earth can they gain by sinking the *Arabic?* Gott and the Kaiser alone know.

Tonight my transfer is in Orders and tomorrow I move. I will send the address immediately I get it. I shall miss the draft leaving for France right away.

7.55 A.M. Tuesday, 9 November, '15.

Dearie: —

Your letter came — to use the novelist's expression — at the psychological moment (only they spell it differently). Anyhow, it was the one thing needed and, if you promise not to laugh, I'll tell you — I slept with it in my hand (till it fell out). You'll be surprised, of course, but this is being written in Bed 1, Ward 15, No. 2 General Hospital, Chelsea, London.

Don't get excited. I was never better in my life — never. I feel just great; I've just had my temperature taken and all is well. On the sheet above my cot, it says I am suffering from rheumatic cold (whatever that is) and generally run down. Anyhow, as I said, I feel fine, and your letter has done me worlds of good. I'll tell you all about the hospital, if you like. . . .

It's an English hospital; it used to be a college, St. Mark's. Luckily I struck the Australian ward. There are only two English in it: one in the opposite corner as I write — he's screened off — cashing in.

The other is a sixteen-year-old boy of the "cissie" class — a real sport. The rest are Australians and New Zealanders and me — Canuck. Only three can get up. Every day, ladies call in autos and taxis to take out those who can go; they take 'em everywhere, shows and everything. I had no idea that the women of the country were so eager to help. It's splendid.

The place of course is spotless — lots of flowers and a canary bird. It's peaceful, and I guess it's doing me no end of good.

It's peaceful, dear. But — at night — well — most stories have two sides.

The man in the corner dies very slowly.

All the others are wounded — and I guess their wounds hurt more at night.

There is another thing. I guess I've made up my mind I'm going to France alright. But —

It's a very different thing, this volunteering to go now, to volunteering in Ottawa. The brass band accompaniment has all gone. The glamour has worn off. I want to go home. I'd give the world to go home. . . .

Yet, I feel somehow I ought to go.

Night.

Before I go to bed, I want to give you an account of the concert I went to tonight. To begin with, I want to tell you that every other night the greatest concerts you could get are given here. A large number of the best theatrical people live in Chelsea, and on their way to the theatre, they make up parties of their friends and arrange a quick concert in this hospital. It's just great of them, I think.

When I got in the hall, I fairly gasped. If only you could have been there! Imagine the large hall of the college, huge, high, magnificent. Ranged all up and down round the walls, in rows, cots with wounded in them. Between the beds, little benches full of men in blue suits, and Red Cross nurses here, there and everywhere. Round, above, a balcony, also packed with blue-suited men with nurses, and where there was not room on the benches, men sat on the beds — men from all the ends of the earth, of all classes, yet all pals, bound together for one purpose, one end. The air was blue with smoke. At one end was a stage with a lot of the ward screens—folding ones—on it, and an electric lamp or two. I think it was the most impressive sight I've ever seen. Wheeled chairs everywhere, men in every state of bandaged injury, and the men lying in bed, some in dressing gowns, men in silk pyjamas, men in college blazers, and even men in Canadian sweaters.

I shall never forget it, never.

One thing that impressed me was in leaving. You know how a usual crowd of men rush out of a show. Well, this show did not rush—each man dared not touch his neighbour. He did not know where he was hurt.

9.45 A.M. 11 November, '15.

My dearest girl.

. . . Last night, Wednesday, was Zepp. night; but none came. It's curious how methodical the Germans are, even in war. It seems they cannot get away from it. In the trenches in France, I am told they begin their morning and evening "Hate" in the shape of a tremendous artillery bombardment at exactly the same hour to the minute, morning and evening, and stop at the same time. It's curious. You'd think they'd stand a better chance, if they varied it. Wednesday night, in London, is always Zepp. night. Last night, from the windows of the ward, we could see the searchlights, one talking continuously in code to the aeroplanes aloft. Sister said the planes, circling around all night, continuously dropped green rockets — apparently to say all was well.

London, of course, is almost quite dark now, at night. It's a fearful undertaking, crossing a busy street after dark. All the trains have blinds down. The street cars and 'buses are dark inside. Clock faces are not lit up. Of course, there are no electric signs. All shop windows have blinds down.

London has adopted the German plan of displaying captured guns. It's a good idea, I think. I wonder they haven't done it before.

I don't profess to understand the war news these days; I don't know whether it's good or bad. The only thing I do understand, is, that if it hadn't been for the navy, we'd 'a' been licked long ago.

As a matter of fact, I'm absolutely fed up with it all. When I read the American magazines — or rather read the ads. — I just *ache* to be back. I found some new "Penrod" stories, and also some "Wallingford" ones. Oh! Gee! but it's fine to read something live again! I've got hold of a book called "Queed"; I've heard of it somewhere, but I can't think where. I've only read two or three pages, but it looks promising.

No dearie, no England for mine, not without you! To live here in the same conditions as we would be living in the States — No, thank you! Mind you, I want to come back. There's something will always drag me back; but always it will grow stale. I understand that's how it affects all Englishmen who have travelled a bit. Doesn't Kipling say something about it? Methinks —

> "The breezes of England are stale
> And the sunshine of England is pale."

I forget it. Anyhow it hits the spot, as all Kipling's stuff does.

Friday, 8.45 a.m. (In Bed)

I am writing this while they are cleaning up the ward. All the beds are moved around, floor polished, your little table washed — everything made spotless under the watchful eye of Sister. This is done every morning, and when all is shipshape and peaceful again, the doctor comes around. Most of us read. One man makes wire and bead butterflies, which visitors buy off him. Some are not well enough to do anything but lie and doze all day. It's very clean, peaceful and — yes — I guess it is rather nice. The fact is, I feel so awfully fit, I could push a 'bus over with one hand. Yet this morning I am going to have my first electric bath. The boys who have had them say they are rather nice.

It's a regular old London November fog outside, yellow, soapy. Yet, somehow, London —

and fascinating. It sneaks through the cracks in the windows, under the doors, everywhere. Dear old, dirty London! I am sick of her. — Yes. But from the ends of the earth I have to come back, and again back. She's irresistible.

Yet I hate the very sound of the English accent. I am absolutely an American in all the word stands for. I don't like the English — *But* — There it is — Just this one town has "got me" and will always have, as it has all Englishmen who have lived here, from the North Pole to the South. Just give me a steerage ticket across the Atlantic, and without a cent I would fairly run on board. . . .

Monday, 9 A.M.

I mentioned, I think, how the rich people send crates full of fruit for this hospital, from the Queen downwards. Well, now a contrast: a parson came in the other night with a small parcel under his arm. He said a poor girl in the East End had been denying herself sugar for two months, so the wounded soldiers could have it. There were perhaps two pounds. Pathetic, eh.?

In this war, you get a good chance to see what a leveller this war is from a social point of view. A woman with about a thousand pounds' worth of furs sits on one bed, and the next holds a poor woman from the East End who has done her very best to trick herself out a bit, and only made herself look pathetic. Of course in Canada, or the States, the gulf is not so wide; but here where it has been, and will be again, so wide as to be unbridgeable, indeed a separate world altogether, it strikes with tremendous force. The men all look alike, in bed or in a blue hospital suit. Only when they speak can you place them; but their visitors label 'em at once and forever. I notice the men in the poorer class kiss their sons. The rich don't. The poor display all their emotions from joy to tears. The rich seem casual, offhand, just pleasantly cheery. But —

I know there are no serious heart-to-heart talks in this; but I don't feel like that kind of a talk. Let it rest a while, till I get out of here.

Friday, 19 November, '15.
No. 2 General Hospital,
Chelsea, London.

. . . I was only thinking, last night, I'm having one of the times of my life: lots of the best grub, all kinds of good shows to see, nothing to do, and a couple of Sisters running around fixing you up all the time, a comfy bed, and lovely clean things every other day — and all the time feeling absolutely fine. I forgot to mention that a masseuse gives me electric air baths every other day, which are just too great for anything —and this is War. Gee !

The lady I mentioned in the previous letter,

who I got the chocolates from, was a multi-millionaire. She brings a big six Rolls-Royce limousine with her and puts all the boys in she can get, and sends her chauffeur along to drive 'em all over London, while she stays in the ward and sews buttons on the boys' shirts for 'em. She is getting up a sort of bazaar. Every man in this place has to *make* something. Prizes will be given, and the things sold as souvenirs, the money to go to the Red Cross. It's great fun. We all have something. Some of the boys here are knitting scarfs, string bags, dressing dolls. You'd die to see some of the results. I have a kettle holder to make. It's a kind of a square piece of canvas with holes in it. In the middle is a cat, and I have to fill all the little holes in it with wool. It's awful hard work, and I guess I'm making a rotten mess of it. But, as I said, it's a lot of fun. . . .

I forgot whether I told you that this hospital has the record for London of turning out ninety per cent, of its casualties cured. They are very jealous of their reputation, and it's harder to get out than it is in. They don't want to take any chances.

We were to have had that boat-load of wounded from the *Anglia,* but you know what happened most of them — so last night we got a train from the Dardanelles. . . .

About noon. Sister asked me if I'd like to go out in the afternoon. You bet I did. A lady came with a six Rolls-Royce limousine and took all the car would hold to Kingsway Hall to a concert. - After the concert she took us to tea.

Gee, but the Londoners have changed; this war sure has given them a jolt. Just imagine a year or two ago what would happen if a bunch of fellows strolled into the stalls of a show in dressing gowns — in dear, staid old London! And yet I've seen that happen, and seen fellows carried in at full length, and every one anxious to help. Once, to applaud a turn was vulgar. Today all the cat calls, whistles, and roars to come back are quite in order, and only just draw pleasant, indulgent smiles from the one-time stiff people of a few years ago. The common or garden Tommy owns London today, and the people are finding out what Kipling told them a few years ago : that he is just an ordinary man "most remarkable like you." You must realize that before the war a Tommy in uniform was not even allowed in a better part of the theatre or in the best bars of the West End hotels.

It struck me yesterday that England may perhaps be different, after all, when the war is over. There were several ladies yesterday with parties of fellows, and one thing I could not help noticing — that all that patronising way that the "upper" classes always affected when giving charity, was all gone. They honestly got down to brass tacks, and meant everything, and enjoyed doing it. If only that get-together Reeling would last, England would be the finest country in the world. At tea, which we had in one of the side rooms in the hall, we were waited on by the ladies who took us and by the people who sang and played. One party was being waited on by Lord Kitchener's sister.

And now I must quit and get on with my cat, which my Canuck lady says is very good and should have a prize. Ahem !!!!

Tuesday, 13 December.

You'll want to hear about the Zepp. raid. All the town is on edge now. The barber, as he shaves you, says he knows for a fact six are on the way now; we are to have them every night. The news boys ask you about them; every one you speak to discusses nothing else. You see it was the first time the war got "right home." They've had Zepp. raids on London, of course, before; but never three of 'em right overhead in the West End—the pleasure part—with anti-aircraft guns banging from the most unexpected places, some throwing star shells, others shrapnel, others high explosives—and the long silver streak dropping her death and destruction all around, apparently oblivious of all the attempts to bring her down. Crowds blocked the streets and yelled, collaring hold of each other as a shell burst right over the machine. Every time she dipped in her manœuvres, which were most remarkably graceful and rapid for such a huge affair, they thought she was coming down, and roared like at some huge firework display. It was the most stupendous show I shall ever see. I was tremendously lucky. When I first heard the banging, I was on the Y. steps, talking to a Yank who had joined the English army. We saw the thing as soon as the searchlights found her, and raced towards her. She was headed our way at the time, and when right over us, there was a rushing sound overhead and a hell of a bang which seemed right on top of us. In reality, the bomb had fallen about thirty or forty yards away on the corner of a saloon which it tore completely away, entering the ground and breaking open a gas main. This took fire and a flame shot 'way up over the house tops, busted windows all around, dropped bits of glass on us. I thought it was parts of a shell and I had got it this time; but I hardly felt it. The heat from the gas burning was tremendous. Lots of people running aimlessly and yelling. I never saw my Yank friend again, but an Australian officer came up—the police were quite helpless, so he and I got one of those barrels they put street refuse in—a yellow three-wheeled thing. We found some sand in a big green bin on the corner and filled her up—the barrel, I mean—and chucked the whole works on the hole where the flames came up. A teaspoonful would have done as much good. By this time a crowd was there, mostly soldiers. Then came a fire engine. The Australian had one end of the big nozzle; I was next. The soldiers all lined up and formed a fatigue. It was great. The firemen went to bust walls and things to get back of the saloon, as it was on fire, too. All we did was to hold the nozzle over the hole in the street, as near to it as we could get, but it didn't put it out. The Zepp. was sailing merrily around all the time, absolutely oblivious of the guns — the shooting was a joke — and every one was saying "where are the aeroplanes.?" But narry a one went up. I had a row with a Royal Flying Corpsman about it. He said they hadn't enough machines. Damn rot! Some one blundered over that raid; they've admitted it, as a squad of French airmen have come to town and they've mounted bigger guns here and there.

Later (just been down to tea).

By the way, this is a rotten place to write. I'm in the big main hall. It's packed — soldiers of all kinds from the ends of the earth. In the morning, this same hall will be full of sleeping soldiers, wounded and others, on the sofas and things. They cannot find beds anywhere. I sleep in a large dormitory that was once the main smoking-room, now full of iron cots. No distinction is made. We are all the same. My God, to think I nearly forbore to wear this khaki! I would have died of shame. . . . Thank God, I am in it, and—dearie—remember it is all done in your name—yours—and Billie's, who is half English. But to resume on the raid—I have lost the thread, I must look up where I left off. Yes, bigger guns, and that reminds me I have a cutting. Wait . . .

To come to the horrid, yet most serious part. Of course, though they smashed a lot of property, they did no real damage. It is also—about—true that they never kill a soldier. But you don't want to believe what you read about the "casualties."

This particular night, they didn't have enough ambulances. That's true. An archdeacon preached a sermon, last Sunday, in which he said he personally knew five babies that were blown to bits.

I myself saw so many bodies being carted away that I didn't bother to count them.

I heard from a soldier eye-witness where they had to jump over lots of dead bodies to get to work on a burning building. The bomb had dropped on a crowd.

One story told me in the Y. here was about a motor-bus driver's head dropping into an adjacent street. I think it was true, though of course it seems fantastic.

I suppose it's war alright. They talk of war on women and babes; but, damn it, we should do the same. Why not? Where is our gas, etc. ? But, if we can win without it, I'd be more pleased if we could and would "play the game."

7 January, '16.

Moved into new billets with two good boys, both very nice. We are all in one room, nineteen in the house altogether. Our window overlooks the sea. Feel very pleased with everything, just old lady—young son, boy scout—got breakfast for all of us this morning. Mother sick. Helped him at night to wash dishes—Awfully nice kid.

Yesterday met a man going blind with ptomaine poisoning. Gave him note to Lai— seemed awfully strange sending messages like that, made the distance between us seem closer, and yet, oh, so far away.

In my heart, I don't think I'll be home next Xmas. I don't think this war will be completed by then, and again when it's over they can't ship every one over inside six months. It's Hell; but it's better to face it than kid yourself.

20 January, '16.

Volunteered for draft in afternoon. Passed doctor in good shape. Feel greatly relieved and bucked up that I have managed to get on. Draft consists of fifty men. As we are practically all strangers to each other, it is a little "difficult" at first, but no doubt that will soon rub off. The office staff volunteered in great style; the whole postal department volunteered in a body.

Got a new kit — quality not nearly so good as the original one received in Ottawa.

21 January, '16.

Paraded for inspection before the Colonel — all O.K. He said "Men, you all look fit and well, and are about to have the chance you have waited for — etc. etc." Still have no definite idea of our destination.

Weather very wet and miserable. Crossing will not be much fun — sea high.

Taking only just what kit I really need. Leaving the rest in my billet till I return.

22 January, '16.

Wet and cold. Went for route march, feel great. Told were sure to leave any minute now. Hope so — don't like the suspense. Had lectures again from ten-thirty. The more I see there is to know, the more scared I get. All the fellows but a few learned something or other while in training in Canada, and more here. All I know is the Army Office routine, or that part of it directly connected with the Records, which

I am afraid will not amount to much in the field. However, guess I can learn.

I want to put you wise again to that so-called "casualty" who will call on you — the one that's going blind. Be sure you don't do anything for him twice. I heard last night he was in the habit of saying he got his trouble at Festubert from gas, and then "touched" you for half a dollar.

Sunday. (Noon)

Still here, glorious day, sun shining, warm as spring. Just been for a stroll along the prom. Sea splashing right on to the board walk. Ten A.M. paraded with overseas party for church — went to Congregational (no option). In the whole church there were just three women, no civilians, two officers, and tucked away at one side was our party. I can't understand the reason. If we hadn't blown in accidentally, the congregation would have consisted of five persons.

I don't like the service at all. It's the first time I've been to a church of that kind, I think.

I have found quite a different outlook on everything since I got away from the city side of things; I have a "job of work" to do. It will last so long and no longer, and the only thing to do is to make the best of it till I can come home.

It is my intention to slip this into an envelope at the last minute. That minute may be tonight.

We parade at seven p.m., so excuse any sudden ending. Had identification tag stamped. Hope I can hang on to it for you as a souvenir. Fellows are wearing them as bracelets now, instead of around neck.

Told we could not take cameras or keep diaries. Shall chance diary, but be careful what I enter. Weather getting worse. Don't think we shall go this week, personally.

Beds all torn up. Place now mess room for troops, long oilcloth-covered tables run up and down the floor from the stage to the back; ticket offices, cloak room, etc. form kitchens. Strikes one as very novel, on first entrance, to see men peeling spuds in the ladies' cloak room, makes very good place for lectures. Was told what was expected of us and so forth (apparently there's quite a lot). No one knows where we are going or just when, but we must not leave billets. So it's any minute. Completed all kit packing (awful job!) but have everything in fine shape now.

Feeling tremendously well.

Quite confident you will approve of my action. . . .

II
AT THE BASE

II

AT THE BASE

Thursday, 29 January, '16.
(Address as usual)

My very dearest girl: —

Today there was an "Overseas Draft" wanted — I volunteered — was accepted — passed the doctor with flying colours. He said I was in splendid shape.

Tonight I get my kit—and tomorrow I begin my real—really work—the kind you will be proud of.

I shall write every slightest opportunity.

Wish me luck!

Another letter tomorrow.

Your own loving pal and husband,

R. A. L.

4 February, '16.
Somewhere in France.

My very dearest Lal: —

Arrived in camp here safely and am now waiting orders to move up the line.

Just when I have the most interesting things to tell you, I must confine myself to generalities, so you must understand, when you get letters which contain nothing but uninteresting personal details, that it is not my fault.

The weather here is not bad, but damp and cold. We are in tents (twelve in each) out in the country, and the work is just fatigues, etc. until we get attached permanently to some particular detail. This morning I helped scrub out the Y.M.C.A hut. *Some* job, and I'm afraid I'm not very expert at it as yet.

The camp here is about the cleanest and best arranged I have seen. Of course, everything is much stricter — discipline and everything. It's very obvious that there is a war on.

I don't think there is any more I can tell you. It isn't much; is it? But I'll write more, when I get settled. I hope you won't forget to write oftener now; will you ?

Give my love to Bill. With every best thing I can wish for you.

Sunday Afternoon, 5 February, '16.

My dearest Lal: —

. . . We are still in the same camp at the base, waiting instructions, and I shall be glad when we move. There's nothing to do but fatigues all day, and it's getting monotonous. There's a big English camp quite close, and we have (at least our outfit has) to go up there all the time, filling trucks with supplies. There's a little wee railroad system — narrow gauge — which apparently takes the supplies to different units. You generally get through about 7.30. The meals are rotten — the boys who have been up the line say it's fifty times better up there. However, I guess it's all in the game; anyhow, I feel most awfully fit. Last night, there was a concert at the Y. presided over by a chaplain — I don't know his name, but he's about the best type of parson I've seen for a long time — no hot air — seems to understand just what's wanted. I heard a fellow say that if more parsons were like him, there'd be a jolly lot more fellows go to church, and I heartily agree.

Today, we all had to attend church in a cinema building over in the English camp — C. of E. service. — The sermon was quite uninteresting. It's amazing how a man can go through life without getting in close touch with his fellow men. This particular man was utterly out of his element preaching to a bunch of Canadians on active service. . . .

Remember always I am thinking of you.

13 February, '16.
No. 3. Canadian General Hospital,
B. E. F.

My dearest Lal: —

At last I can write to tell you I am settled — at least for some time, and believe me it is some relief after knocking around since Christmas Eve. . . . We left England quite a large bunch, but are now split up, a few here and there to different corps. It was rather hard on some of the fellows, particularly those who had joined from some small town in Canada together, kept together right along, and then were finally separated. Being with any one you know well makes all the difference in strange camps, though where we are now, every one seems to be so jolly decent that it doesn't matter so much.

Right up to the time when we left Sandgate, I was getting more and more disgusted with things. There seemed nothing definite about the work, nothing to tie to. Even the work in London was more or less unsettled. I began to think all I had heard about decent corps coming over must have been a myth, but at last it seems I have drawn the right thing — something worth taking a real interest in and something incidentally to be proud of, as undoubtedly this corps is about the best of its kind that has come out here. I haven't started any regular work yet, but expect to tomorrow (Monday). I don't know what it will be, either, but I suppose the usual thing in a big hospital. Of course it is all Canadian. The Y.M.C.A. hut where I am writing is quite a different one to the usual run. I understand it was organized before the fellows left Montreal. It's a private one and right on the ground, very quiet, very clean, and altogether nice in every way. There is a piano of course, heaps of papers, magazines and so forth, and a first-rate library, also lots of comfy chairs.

The usual run of camp Y.'s are — as far as I saw — just grocery stores, and only open at stated hours. That one at our last stopping place was a terror — you stood in line waiting your turn to get in sometimes for half an hour or so; to sit down was quite an event. There was a concert every night, it's true, and the chaplain was one of the finest men I have ever met; but as a place to rest or read or write it was impossible. The men have their own mess, the first I have struck. It costs five francs only, a month. Another thing which is fine, you can go down town without a pass. It means I suppose they can trust a fellow, which is rather more than nice.

There are a great many things I want to say to you, but one rather hates to get personal in a censored letter. Twice a month we get issued with a green envelope. You are on honour not to put anything of military significance in it, or rather write anything and enclose it. So when the "Postie" hands you those, you want to look out as the contents will be uncensored.

23 February, '16.

My very dearest Lal: —

This is positively the first time I have had a chance to write you since the first letter after my arrival here. I thought there would be a lot of time for reading and writing, but when the day's work is done, you're so nearly all in that to get down between the blankets seems the only thing you can do. I'll try and tell you all about things.

Firstly—you mustn't get the impression that, because I am in France, I am necessarily in the thick of things. I am far, far safer here than in England for that matter. In London there was always the mild excitement of a Zepp. raid—and the rather intense excitement of dodging taxicabs, while crossing the streets at night.

Here if a Zepp. passes over—which I don't suppose ever happens—it doesn't condescend to notice us. Even to see an aeroplane is a novelty, and "the line" might be a million miles away, for all we see of it.

My work is just plain work—lots and lots and lots of it—and then some. At seven a.m. I go on duty in my ward. At seven p.m. I come off. In case this might get monotonous, every other night I "stand to" to take in the wounded. At other times I sleep.

Of course this was not a real hospital in the first place. My ward happens to be in a building. The rest are huts exactly similar to the huts you have seen pictured in Canada and other papers.

We have forty-five beds; two orderlies, three sisters and a fourth-year McGill man do all the work. We are situated up-stairs. In one sense, it's a nuisance because of the perpetual carrying;

but in another it's better because they don't put many stretcher cases there for fear of fire, so most cases can walk and help around the ward a bit—and the first duty of an orderly is to get "jake" with the patients and put 'em to work without raising too many kicks. I guess you might like to know a few details of the work. At six reveille goes, and half dopey you crawl out of bed (we sleep on the floor on a sort of loft place); six-thirty breakfast in the dining-room, seven roll-call and "break away" to the patients' kitchen. Here you wait, at a counter, your turn to get the pans of bacon or porridge and the two pails of tea which is their breakfast. Fortunately my ward is not far from the kitchen—some are the deuce of a way as this is a very big hospital. When you arrive up-stairs, you dish out in a little back attic—which we call our kitchen—the grub for each patient. Those who can, help you. The night orderly has put out the tea bowls on each locker and cut the bread and butter. This done, there is water to be fetched—no water is laid on—and that one short remark should convey a lot to you. You can guess how much we use. We haven't a boiler and what isn't heated up on the round iron stoves in the two wards, has to be done on a wee alcohol stove just like the one we had at home.

Well, I get water, heat it and put a bunch of patients to work washing up, others to sweeping.

Then I beat it for the coal. (All these things I "beat it" for, remember, have to be carried upstairs as well as some distance away.) After I have fixed the stoves and the coal, I hustle away with the dirty water and the garbage to the incinerator; and, in between carrying endless pails of water, I get the day's drugs, bandages, stores, extras and about a million other things. At about ten, I put some guys to work cutting bread for dinner. At ten-fifty I go and draw it— serve it— and so forth. Don't forget forty-five dinners is quite a job to handle. They are darn good dinners, too—lots of it. The "afternoon"— each man, chocolate, cigarettes, matches, oranges—and so forth. (The ones who help get a bit of extra here.) At three-fifty it's tea time, eggs (2), same old bread and butter job, washing up, etc. Then at 6 draw men's rations, bread— butter—sugar, get the night orderly's water—or some of it, and generally leave everything "jake" by 7 p.m.—*then bed.* (There are lots of duties— not all pleasant—I haven't mentioned.)

I guess you are thinking I hate it. Well, if so, you'll be wrong—I don't.

To begin with, the McGill man and the other orderly, a qualified trained nurse, are both *fine* (gentlemen, of course) and we pull together well.

But the whole thing depends on the Sisters,— whether they are grouchy. Our three, also the night Sister, are just great, so there is no friction anywhere. There is so much work to do, and we all dig in and do it.

I have done things I never believed I could possibly do — and liked it. . . . I have seen wounds that you cannot bear to look at — explosive bullets which go in like any other bullet, but come out leaving a hole you can get your fist in.

But I am not going to tell you about all that. It just amounts to this; that any one who would kick at having to wait on and work for these fellows, after what they have gone through, isn't worth much.

I have mentioned that every other night I helped take in cases.

The Staff is divided into two sections A. and B. One is on one night, and one the next. The work goes like this:

At any hour during the night you must be prepared to stand to, within five minutes of the call. Roll is called and, half asleep, shivering with cold, you march over to the Receiving Room and wait outside the door. The Receiving Room is all lit up. Down the middle are rows of tables for the clerks to take the names of, and all particulars of, the men as they come in. At one table are the doctors. Usually the first to arrive, come in a big motor 'bus — the "sitters" — and believe me a fellow has to have it bad to get a stretcher. As the motor draws up to the door, the party known as the stretcher party rushes up and helps them out and over to the Receiving Room to get their particulars and assign them to wards. After they're assigned, a man takes them over. (I'll tell you the next part later. I don't work at the Receiving Room since I've had a ward.) To my mind, the unloading of the "sitters" is more pathetic than the arrival of the stretcher cases. They come looking deathly ill, in the electric glare—just with the rough dressings they got up the line. Nearly all are plastered with yellow mud, where they have lain. Some have hardly any clothes. All have just any old uniform at all—The very antithesis of a peace soldier— None have slept since God knows when—yet they all attempt to be cheerful. It's either inspiring or dreadful, whichever way your nature makes you look at it. No matter how bad they've got it or how little, to me it is fine and wonderful to be able to help them when they are here.

Very soon the ambulances come creeping up out of the night, up to the door. All is well-ordered hustle—no noise but the purring of the motors and the "Got him.?" "Go ahead", of the stretcher-bearers as they lift them out of the car. Each one contains four. I was desperately afraid I should drop my first one, but I soon got used to it.

When you have got your case, you—as gently as you can—take him inside and put him on the floor where he is interrogated as to his regiment, name, etc. His wound particulars are entered on a card which is tied to his uniform up the line. Some, of course, are not able to say anything. When a ward is assigned, two other fellows carry him there.

This goes on till all have arrived, when the bunch go off to bed.

Usually hot cocoa is given the fellows while on this work, which helps some, as the nights are raw and cold. (Today we have snow, though the trees are all in bud.) ...

If you are an orderly, when the fall-in sounds, you beat it to your ward. Here all is quiet hustle, getting night-shirts around the stoves, boiling up Oxo, preparing beds, getting out Blues for the patients to wear, and putting pans of hot water on a form with towels, soap etc., as each patient has to be washed before he is put to bed.

Immediately the man brings along the patient assigned you, you jump to get his clothes off him. Sometimes this is quite a job. (Most of them of course are — well — lousy.) You chuck the clothes in a corner to be taken to a fumigator, giving the man his personal stuff, his hat, and his boots. Then you wash him — at least that part of him out of bandages, then take him to bed and give him a bowl of Oxo. Sometimes you have about 4 or 5, all washing at once and you are rushed like the deuce. I have known men to go to sleep during the process. When all are in bed, you go, too—till 6 A.M.

Nearly all our patients are English Tommies. They are of every possible type and condition, but they all look the same to us, and they all get anything we can give 'em. Class prejudice doesn't go here, and we have no use for a grouch.

The first question a patient asks you most eagerly, "Is it a Blighty wound?" That means one bad enough to be sent to England, yet not bad enough to keep here. The "nice" wounds are the Blighty ones.

Next day, most of 'em just lie and sleep, but each day they get brighter and brighter. Usually the first sign of recovery is when they begin to kid the orderlies and the Sisters, and ask "Ay, chum, 'ave you got a bit more bread and butter ?" The answer is always *yes*. We give 'em all they want.

They sure like the Can"*ai*"dians.

Everything is done on a system. Those with shrapnel or bullets in 'em go down next day to be X-Raved. Next day, it's taken out and handed to them. It's just an everyday business.

26 February, '16.

. . . I do not exaggerate when I tell you that I do not sit down, not even to meals, which I snatch standing up in between washing dishes from six A.M. to about now—eight p.m. There isn't time. When the doctor comes in the morning, I help with the dressings, such as holding an arm with a double fracture, where a bullet has torn a hole that you can see right through, while the doctor cleanses it and dresses it. At one time not so long ago, it would have made me sick in the tummy. It doesn't now any more; my nerves are jake — I am my own man. . . .

So Wilson is going to help strafe our friends a bit. I am sorry for the same reason you are. Bill was with you when you were writing. How I would love to see her and play with her, and to teach her to like her old dad. Home doesn't seem so far away after your letters, but it pulls at my heart strings as I could never have believed possible— But — all may have been for the best. Oh, if only the war would end! But I am afraid that — terribly afraid — it is to be of long duration. Do you remember how every one was so optimistic at the beginning. I prophesied the coming October; I wish it was to be true: But — ?

27 February. (Sunday Evening)

My dearie: —

It's Sunday evening. I guess our occupations are very different — Just the same we can talk in the same old way. Since I got your letter last night, I have felt great, all day. It's fine to think that although so far away and on such strange work, I have my one real pal to talk to in the same old way, the one person who will understand *thoroughly,* and, I hope, sympathize.

I wrote last night telling you of the new condition of my work under quarantine. Today of course has been just the same round of work — if anything just a bit more interesting — as I am beginning to be entrusted with bandaging after the doctor has put on the dressings, and gone on to the next case where I have previously cut away the bandages of the day before. They're all progressing very favourably. . . . Gee, but they're a funny crowd, those English! Their peculiar idea of humour and their conversation is the limit. None of them can get over the fact that the Canadians get "four bob and a tanner" a day. In the bottom of their hearts, they think that is the main reason we join. Not in a million years could they grasp it that these — McGill men and all — are not ordinary working men like themselves. One fellow said today in his peculiar North Country accent:

"'T' Canadians ain't done nowt since Eeeps — ony road." And another, "Aai, and got fower bob a day for doing of it."

Some are grateful for every little thing; others won't even say *thank you* for every possible attention. The only successful way to get on with 'em (and make 'em work) is to practise a philosophical kind of cheerful kidding manner. And, more you

have to kid yourself. If you let things worry you
or take any notice of them when they kick, your
life would be hell. . . .

France, 29 February, '16.

(Say, this is leap year, eh.")

(You may have wondered that, if we get only
two green envelopes a month, how the dickens
all of my letters come in these treasured
receptacles. Answer—I buy 'em at half a franc
jper from the English Tommies and am charging
it up to you. At present you owe me one fr. fifty.)

My dearie:—

It's afternoon. All the dishes—pots, I mean—
are washed up, the ward swept and all looks
clean and fresh and tidy. . . . (I dunno whether I
am disclosing information of military importance to the enemy in the green envelope, if I tell
you that this place was once a Jesuit College,
very old apparently, with high walls round, and
no modern conveniences till we came. It makes
a fairly good hospital, I think.) . . .

I think you'll be pleased to hear I am "making
good"—if you can use such a large phrase in
connection with such a small job. You must
realize that only a short while ago I positively
could not have done this work at all. I can't
even now realize that it is me doing some of the
things I have to do—and not kicking at it. I never

even touched a wounded person before, but now I have—But wait, I'll tell you the proceedings. About ten a.m. the doctor (a captain) comes, puts on a white coat and rubber gloves, and prepares to do the dressings. First I go ahead to each bed and with a pair of scissors usually cut— or untie in some cases—the bandages from the first case he intends fixing up. These I chuck in a pail of water and between us the Sister and I hand the various dopes. When he is through, he moves to the next, and one of us bandages it up again. (I never put a bandage on before, but today I did nearly all.) While I was holding a particularly bad wound and fracture (to drop it would probably mean it would fall to pieces) I was congratulated on the way I did the work. The sight etc. close at one time, would have sickened me, but now my only feeling is one of interest. I don't think you have ever been in a surgical ward, have you? Everything has to be done with the minutest care, everything must be absolutely sterile. To put a pair of forceps, scissors, anything even, on the table makes it un-sterile and it cannot be used. Everything you hand the doctor, you hand with forceps. Your mind has to be on your job every fraction of the second; your nerves must be as steady as a rock. Can you see me doing it? *And* doing it alright. Sister says she's going to give me all that kind of work she can. Of course the other orderly does this at any other time, but he is barred out of the ward until quarantine is lifted. Of course, I do all the other work as well: clean up, dish out the meals — everything. I sure have landed myself on some job, yet I like it.

I have more than once wanted to go up the line — and I want to tell you about it. Right now, I'd love to go. I have tried to analyse my feelings. I want to go up and see it all first hand, I know exactly what the work is — but I want to see it. — I do want to see you and Billy. That about explains it. Of course if I hadn't Bill and you, I would go tomorrow. But — I repeat — I want to come home. . . .

As regards the actual work — I'm " doing my bit" more here than I would be there.

By the way, I was comparing this Canadian Gen. Hosp. with the English one. They're utterly different. Here there are no visitors, no automobile rides, no shows. *But* — for arrangement, order, efficiency, Canada has 'em strung forty ways. There isn't any comparison. (Afterwards you will see McGill come in for some pretty high praise. You see if I'm not right.)

The Sisters and doctors are *human* — they treat the patients as men, that's one big difference and a very big one. The grub is far better — the Tommies nearly had a fit to find *two* eggs to a meal. Every day there is a package of smokes for every man, and chocolate and fruit, all from Canadians at home. Most of the packages have ready addressed P.C.'s so that the fellows can thank the donors if they wish, and I have impressed it on them that they have got to be returned. The English Tommy is not much at writing to a stranger. Sometimes I write P.C.'s for fellows to their own people. Gee! it's pathetic. "I hope this finds you as it leaves me at present," etc. They are so different to Americans. Nearly all the eggs, for instance, have messages on them and addresses—quite a lot from girls' schools. Yet the fellows are too shy to drop a jolly card, I bet not one would go unanswered from the States. . . .

10 March, '16.

My dearest Lallie: —

This will not be a long letter—just a note telling you I am K.O. and everything going well with me. . . .

Things are—I would have thought at one time—the limit; but at times like these, and given a bunch who work together, the almost impossible can be done, if done with a will.

We came out of quarantine K.O. No more cases of fever. All the boys were sent off to C.C. or B.D. (Base Details—waiting to go back up to the front.) Immediately we evacuated, we filled up, and I was still alone in two wards.

I wish I might tell you the details, but I can't—not till *Après la Guerre*. Sufficient maybe when I say that the trenches are full of snow (you'll have seen the English picture papers), and I have had a ward full of men who, having taken a trench from the Germans, owing to certain conditions lost their trench waders in the slush and mud, and fought for thirty-six hours without any boots of any kind. Of course you will understand, without my giving you details about frozen feet. Even then we couldn't keep them — only a while.

Believe me, it's hell up the line these days — and worse is to come.

We haven't our water laid on in my ward yet, and it's upstairs as I told you. But, all the same, we have just everything else for the boys that you can imagine. The water is my personal trouble. What I meant was the men get everything. Thank God, we give 'em all just the same : oranges, eggs, cigarettes. I wonder if the people who subscribe to those things in Canada realize how fine a work they're doing. The other day I sent out a ward full of men on stretchers, and all had bed socks and nearly all pyjamas — every blessed thing a gift from the Canadian Red Cross. Imagine, if you can, a man piled on a stretcher and transferred from the warm ward to motor ambulance, taken through the town streets, then the boat — a bitterly cold crossing, then his long English train journey, then again motor ambulance and lastly his new bed in the English ward. Don't forget it—he suffers alright! And to have given one blessed pair of bed socks, which have helped a fellow on such a trip, is something to comfort yourself with.

The Sisters have sure gone some, too, recently

— and are, this minute. I don't know how they do it and keep up.

Today noon was the first day I have eaten at our mess for three weeks. Quarantine has been over for some days, but I haven't had time to quit for dinner or for tea—I've eaten standing up in the wards. I've been as much as three days without a decent wash. And yesterday I heard (genuine news) our work is to be increased one third. . . .

But that is only the beginning. This war is going to go out, more terrific than it came in.

And now I must beat it. About a million jobs await me.

Always—understand—I am *yours yours yours* — my work is for you, I am for you.

I am your boy and your husband,

R. A. L.

P.S. Kisses for Billie—our Billie eh? She will kiss you for me—give her Dad's love.

20 March, '16, France 1 A.M.

This letter is sure disconnected alright, as I said it would be, but I will finish it off, and send it, because for the next few days I can't write regularly.

The other night I turned out for convoy—luckily nothing doing in our ward, so I beat it for the "hay." I'd no sooner got to sleep, than out I was pitched, to go back and sleep in my ward. Once more I was quarantined—a new fever case. When I arrived, they took off the night man—and there I was, and *am*, alone in my glory with two wards full of "irrespressibles ", as Punch calls 'em, to look after, and can't get out for days. I worked that night, all next day, and now I'm on again tonight—feeling a wee bit "dopey" for want of sleep. I have no night Sister, and no one can come up here. Fortunately everything is going swimmingly and there isn't much to do, but to take a few temperatures now and then, and look out for certain bandages slipping. At seven or eight A.M. I go to bed and will have a Sister (for days only) and she'll have to get patients to clean up, etc. I do seem to find it, don't I? However, each night I'll be able to have a talk with you. I don't have any meals to get at night, only cocoa at eight p.m., and bread and butter; also there don't happen to be any important dressings. I even see where I'll be able to read a bit. For the last hour, I've been reading the *Bystander, Sketch*, and old newspapers, and altogether enjoying myself. At the end of the largest ward is my little kitchen—under the bare tiles I have a stove, electric light, and a collection of canned eats that would make your mouth water.

It's on the kitchen table, on a writing pad that some kind person in Canada has sent for general hospital distribution, that I am writing this. I have the door open a bit so I can hear if all is K.O. in the ward (you'd think it wasn't). Wounded men talk a lot in their sleep. . , .

"Swinging the Lead" is English all over France for the boys who play sick when they are well, to try to get a few more days in Hosp. Down here, it is played quite openly, and is a joke. If the Sister "falls", well and good; if she is "wise", also well and good. Some get away with it, some don't; but it's all in good part, as it can only go a few days at most. The boys "kid" one another openly in front of Sister or the Doctor about this, and sometimes it's very funny.

22 March, '16.
France, 12.30 at night.

My dearest Lal:

You say in your last letter, you feel blue. I often feel so blue for you and our Billie. But, dearie, hold on. This thing can't last, and we shall win, of course — so, — stick it, same as me.

The convoy ambulances buzz, out of the window, all the time. Oh, Lai, who would have thought such things could have been in our life, so short a time ago! And yet — as you say — how fine to take a part, however humble! And even I, surrounded by object lessons, don't begin

to comprehend how things are up the line. I
think I know what things are like pretty well; but
all the time I *don't*. I don't know a thing about
the suffering, the monotony. The fighting is
nothing; it's the continual working, the grind,
grind, grind, and always the casualties, — always
them. When I feel sleepy and inclined to kick, I
think of these boys here in their beds, and the
others on trains or ambulances or lying waiting
in the mud, and then of *you.* . . .

It's cold tonight, there's a tile or two out of
my kitchen roof, and no matter how I keep the
wee American stove *Whoop-up* (from coal which
I have beside it in an American Can concern's
box), it's shivery. I have also forty-seven men's
dishes to wash before dawn, hot water to get, my
own dinner to cook, lots of little things to look
after for the bed patients — and the general look-
out to keep. . . .

1 A.M., 23 March, '16.

I thought for sure I had something to say to
you tonight yet somehow, though I am full to
overflowing with thoughts, I cannot put it — or
them — into words. Again, as you see by the time
above, I am writing just after everything is all
nice and cozy in the wards, and I can at last get a
minute alone with you. . . .

Do you know, Lai, I feel — I feel sort of
"washed   out" — weary — words   won't   come,

I guess I want a change or something. But it makes me so mad. When I am busy with my work, I hear or see something and I say to myself, now tonight I'll tell Lai that; but when "tonight" comes, I am all in, — and dispirited — and cannot find the energy to remember anything.

Yet of course we shall win. The French and Ourselves are a victorious army. It's in the air. It's everywhere. The atmosphere speaks victory.

Yet, — always remember — of course — it was the silent British navy that did it. That was the Ace of Trumps, — and it has not been played yet, though our opponents have known now, for a year, we held it, and it was the winning card.

Have you seen Bairnsfather's book of cartoons? Not in the same class as Raemaker's, of course; yet, on the humorous side, awfully good in their way.

Today I had three letters from patients who had gone back up the line. I am keeping them to show you — one Canuck, two English. It's good to feel they've remembered. If you know of any particular people who make a practice of sending cigarettes, and etc. to boys at the front, I can send addresses of men leaving here to go back, all the time. We issue cigarettes, etc. in the wards every day — practically all the packages contain addressed P.C.'s to the senders, and I know of a good many that have been sent back with thanks. It isn't so much here, though, that kind of thing counts; but after they leave to go back up to the trenches—that's when a fellow needs a pal, and we try to keep in touch. Canada has done splendidly, from what I can see by the gifts that are passed through us; but always there is the need of more. And now when we are coming to the final round, before the knock-out, I hope the energy will, if anything, be redoubled.

What has gone before is as nothing to what is to come. . . .

In South Africa, I worked hard, I *thought;* but just because I took a chance on my life, every other day, and was in the saddle hours on end, that wasn't real work. This is *work,* with no excitement—no relief—and withal no credit. Because at the showdown all our work will be forgotten. But about all that I do not care. All I want is an end—to go home—to you, and to Billie—to *play* with Billie—I am tired—and I want you both. I want a little peace.

But that's now. Tomorrow is another day. And no matter how many days of this are in store, good work shall be done—for you—in your name—by me. And with a jolly good heart.

It's only *sometimes*—I'm tired.

Darling—my heart goes out to you *now.*

8.30 A.M., 29 March, '16. (Pay Day !!!) Good morning, Lal!—

This is an awful time to be writing a letter to one's wife—isn't it! Guess I must have got it bad, after a strenuous night, looking after two wards of wounded men all by my lonesome, to start in to write to a mere girl—and *that* girl—my *wife*—Ye Gods! at nine a.m. of a morning! . . .

Say! the other day you said that we were all getting better for the war and a lot of stuff like that (excuse the description). I see where a large English Daily said that owing to the new stringent rules as to the supply of paper, they could no longer print the list of casualties in full. The next morning the paper appeared with about three inches of one column something like this: " Casualties 600—200 Dead—" and that was all. The whole of the opposite page was devoted to sketches and descriptive matter of a new—restaurant dinner gown ! O tempora ! O mores ! What a state of mind the people must have who run that paper. . . .

By jove, I wish you could see some of the shops here! They are just spiffing—especially the cake shops, "specialty" stores, and jewelers. If I had some money I could just buy the loveliest things for almost nothing—The French sure know how to make pretty jewelry and wrought metal things.

Thanks to the British Navy, all the stores down town run just as usual. The flower shops do business, the meat stores have everything, also as before. In fact, you'd never know there was a war on, if you didn't *know*. Also you never see a young man, and there are many widows. The Canucks are "*O très bon—la la*," believe me, with the Frenchies: more so than the other troops, for some reason.

24 May, Empire Day.

Dear Lal, —

Today is Empire day—do you remember at school the old rhyme—"if you don't give us a holiday we'll all run away"? And later we called it *Empire Day*. I remember as kids we were always taught everywhere to know Queen Victoria as one of the most wonderful persons who ever lived—perfect type of woman and queen. But today I am afraid most of us know she was only a very silly old woman. Some one has recently published a book about her, and I suppose she's now dead long enough for the truth to be told without hurting any one very much. It appears she was always dead set against anything ever being suggested, even, to the detriment of Germany—thought the Kaiser a great friend of England, and in fact was altogether just about the opposite of everything we believed as children. As most everything is. I believe if King Edward, wasn't it? had had no children, "Big Bill" would have been King of England. Maybe I have it wrong, but anyhow it seems to have been a narrow squeak.

I am getting most awfully keen on games and have developed into an ardent baseball fan. There is a league: other Canadian Hosps, A.S.C. etc. We have a great team. . . .

I was glad to hear S——— had joined the Signallers and not the Engineers. It is a much better corps for him in every way. You ask what they do. Well, of course, all that flag-wagging which he will be doing now ceases when he gets out here, though they might do a good bit of it in Shorncliffe. (Imagine how long it would take Fritz to pick off a flag-wagger, when it isn't safe to show a finger over a parapet!) It will, however, put him *au fait* with the code, and help if he should be needed on the telegraph instruments. What he will do, will depend altogether on the circumstances — luck — and proficiency. If I were he, I would study the telegraph instrument hard — wireless, too, if he could. Most signalling is done by telegraph. . . . A lot of his work will be fixing telegraph lines and some are used as "runners." It's a nice decent job all round, and he'll meet a lot of decent young fellows. Yes, I guess he's wild — a bit. He tends that way, and of course coming here won't improve him. It would be lucky if he could land a stripe. Then the little responsibility might steady him; but he's rather young for that. Shorncliffe will do him much harm, as they are not so strict there. I suppose he'll take his leave in London — and all the rest of it. He'll just have to take his chance, and have a fling with the rest. If I had a boy, I shouldn't try to stop him. I'd tell him the risks—and leave it to him. S——— will come out alright, I firmly believe. When he comes to France, things are different; all the rough stuff must go. A "drunk" only draws 28 days No. 1 Field Punishment—with the horrors of being tied up every day. That you may have heard of. You are in the B.E.F. then, not the C.E.F.

Later.

The baseball game was just great, we had two generals in the bleachers, but again we got licked. I wish you could see one of the games—the grounds surrounded with the blue hospital coats and the Sisters' uniforms. The Sisters are good rooters, believe me. The rooting takes a more personal tone than in regular games and includes a man's personal appearance—his uniform—his work—any old thing at all so long as we may get his goat. The utmost keenness is shown by every one. I'm afraid the cricket eleven takes a very back seat; baseball has the whole show.

6 June, '16.

If you recall the news in the papers during these last few days, you'll remember a few things happened to the Canucks up the line—hence no time for letters or anything else but work. Things were sure enough lively for the Pats and the 2d C.M.R's. according to the stories brought down.

By the way, I saw some Signallers amongst them, the first I've seen come in — at least the first I've noticed. . . .

One was attached permanently, owing to deafness caused by shell fire.

It appears a Signaller has the grand-stand view of the war in more or less safety. He sits all day, and all night too I suppose, in a steel-covered dugout. Over his head is strapped a telephone head-piece and he receives messages all the time. That's all they do, lucky beggars ! I wish I were in that corps — they'll see *all the show*. I see them come out after it's over and am told about the "turns", secondhand.

By you get this, the sea battle will be old stuff. Already maybe you know more than I do, but to sum up the main events so far for these months, namely this battle — a mistake has been made in letting Germany get in her story to the world first.

Victors do not run away. Germany did. Beatty held their main fleet till our main fleet came up, and therefore suffered heavily. He prevented their gaining their object; that's all, as we had it here. . . .

I'm on a new job which has, as some of its advantages, two afternoons a week and quit daily at 4 p.m. *Active service*—I *don't* think. Churchill was right, and there should be an alteration as to what constitutes a fighting unit. Convalescents should be doing our work — and the majority of us should be up the line. I am perfectly willing to go at any time, but transfers are forbidden ; so many had been asked for that a General Order came out prohibiting it, excepting in very special cases.

10 June, '16.

Dear Lal, —

We are all to be inoculated again twice. Confounded nuisance. My turn is tonight, then again in ten days. ... In Canada and England, a great fuss is made about forty-eight hours after you're "shot in the arm", but that doesn't go in France, like a jolly lot of other things. At five tonight I am going to see the keenest baseball game ever. A match has been arranged with the other No. 3 Can. Hosp. . . . It's a perfect day — and I feel fairly busting with good health and the joy of being alive.

Now and then something comes down the line in the way of an extraordinary wound. This morning, they drew — with the magnet — part of a Ross rifle bayonet out of a man's shoulder. How did it get there? Shell explosion blew it in, I guess. Maybe it was his own bayonet, maybe some other fellow's in another part of the trench.

Do you realize how much goes on in this hospital? The operating room has four tables. A fair day's work for one doctor is thirty operations. Two stretchers do nothing all day but carry cases to the X-Ray room to locate the exact position of the piece of shell or bullet. Then there are the medical cases. The last few convoys, I have carried a fair sprinkling of Trench Fever cases. While on the subject of "patients"—you know our men now have steel helmets. Well, when you see one with a hole in it, and hear an accompanying "story", don't be too, too awe-struck. It may have been stood on a parapet for Fritz to make a souvenir of it. Gee, what yarns we shall hear after this war!

16 June, '16.

My dearest Lai,—

I left off, I believe, where I was to be inoculated. I had plans of "swinging the lead" and sneaking down to the Y for a long talk with you, a nice quiet read, and altogether a nice easy old day all to myself. Well, "the best laid schemes." The inoculation part was all O. K., done with "neatness and despatch"; but next day, instead of coming down here and having a nice easy time, I was so "all in" I just couldn't get out of bed. . . . It took every one the same way, which for some reason comforts me a little. There's another one coming in ten days.

Well—you "compray " the date of this letter.

I suppose your papers are working overtime

to get issues out—once again the Canucks have had it at Ypres. . . .

And say, Lai, the third battle of Ypres—an old story when you get this—was not—is not, as it's on now—like the first or the second. An artillery fellow told me he couldn't hear his gun fire because of the bursting shells sent over by Fritz—not just for a minute, mind, but for forty-eight hours. How anything lived in the front line, I dunno: but the Canucks got back all they lost, and more to it besides. Gee, it's amazing ! If you could see and hear what I do, you wouldn't believe. They've shelled Ypres town again, and bust the Cloth Hall for fair, this time.

The general opinion seems to be that the troops against them in this scrap are nothing like those in the battle last year—lots of young kids, and many with no heart. The officers are as good, though. One German officer, captured by a fellow I carried, killed or wounded four Canuck officers before getting knocked out and captured himself. Of course our men would have killed him, but didn't have an opportunity. Only when things are very quiet or very very busy are prisoners taken.

There's a man, an Englishman, works here. He was taken prisoner by the Germans. When captured, he had a tin of bully and some biscuits on him. Fritz first ate these, cutting the biscuits into very thin slices and making sandwiches with the bully beef, enjoying the feed — he told me — with the greatest satisfaction. Afterwards, they took every single stitch of clothing off him and turned him loose. When about fifty to one hundred yards away, they all took pot shots at him with their rifles; but he got off with only a few slight wounds, wandered three days and three nights till he fell in with one of our working parties. He's been no use ever since. . . . They did the same thing to a large party of a certain Scotch regiment, killing many. That regiment has taken no prisoners since. This is perfectly true.

Sunday Afternoon, 18 June, '16.

My dear Lal, —

I suppose I don't have to tell you to make you understand what's doing; your newspapers are telling you daily. . . . You know ten times more about this, the third battle of Ypres, than I do; true I have heard a hundred first-hand stories, but by men who are not exactly out on observation tours, men who have been chiefly concerned in keeping alive. One sidelight — I have heard it estimated that Fritz put over in six hours roughly £100,000 — $500,000.00 —worth of shells. I dunno', of course how accurate, or non-accurate, that is; but I don't imagine it can be far out.

Nothing now matters but care of the wounded. Night is the same as day for most of us; yet there is no extra fuss or bother, only a patient, instead of staying here awhile, is evacuated to England almost right away. Maybe he spends a night or two, not more.

Saturday, 24 June, '16.

. . . The weather here is most unsettled and must make plans, at any rate for air reconnaissance and so forth up the line, most difficult to arrange. There has been some more fighting up in the salient, though things have slackened off a bit, I think, from the fierce fighting of what is now called the third battle of Ypres. We, at any rate, are not so busy, although things are not slack by any means. You'll remember gas was used again, and we got a fair proportion of those cases. The cough they have is like no other cough you ever heard — not dry or hard, but as if their throats were full of froth of some sort. It's fearful. . . .

I wish I could see some way of getting out of this unit before the fall. Every one is getting out some way, mostly commissions. Both our sergeant-majors are going — a sergeant-major either makes a unit a great one, or puts it on the bum as far as the fellows are concerned. Luckily we have had two of the best in France; but when they go, I see everything going wrong.

21 July, '16.

Well — comprey the date of this — I read your letters, between carrying stretchers, Sat on a stretcher in the road opposite the Receiving Room. My life now (I couldn't tell you before) is just one long stretcher carrying. Night and day are just the same; there is no break; the hum of the ambulance is with you all the time. Try to imagine the scene — remember the early articles we read together in 1914, of the wounded in the hospitals anywhere — everywhere — how you step over them — how they put them just any place. This big hospital is not a general hospital now, but a Clearing Station. Get that? The recreation hall is full of beds. Every place is full of beds, and the "walkers" — Lord, they're everywhere! There is a difference though, in 1916. In 1914 we were retreating. And now we are advancing. Then the hospitals were not prepared; now everything moves like clockwork. Nothing is missing, the whole thing is a marvel of efficiency. Hundreds of times a day I wish you could see it. . . .

Later.

I guess I didn't ought to continue this letter just now, as I am about all in, and still have twelve hours ahead. All afternoon we have "received" and "evacuated" — sometimes in some wards both at the same time, till you are in danger of picking up a stretcher which has just come and sending him to Blighty by mistake. (*He* would worry — not!)

These are the days when Fritz is trying to regain the trenches he lost to the British. In one case, fellows have told me that three whole divisions came up to recapture one line of trenches held by one division of British. Imagine it—not battalions—divisions. They got 'em, too, in this instance, though even as I write, I guess, we have taken them again. It's all too stupendous for me to describe.—corpses three deep—one can't realize it even when the stories are told by men with their wounds running blood.

One thing impressed me: though this rush is something hardly to be believed if not seen, so perfect is the organization that I noticed each man got his extras—his oranges, his cigarettes, just the same. Another thing; those I have carried—Lord knows how many even in these months—I have never heard one complain. Indeed all are cheery even, and always endeavour to crawl off the stretcher on to the bed, when you reach the ward—with the inevitable cigarette.

As usual the "Walkers" *look* the worst.

Do you remember my once telling you about the pale mud on them all—generally from head to foot—how I noticed it much more in the winter and how it was missing in the summer? Well, I noticed it again today, and it appears that when this division were defending the captured German trenches, Fritz by some means flooded through with water three deep.

One other thing: during the winter and before the "push", all the patients came down *fairly* neatly bandaged and washed. Now the blood stays where it is — except on the wound — and mud and blood are congealed together all over a man. If we're busy, what about the Dressing Stations who send to all the hospitals?

22 July, '16 (Lunch time).

Just got up after strenuous night. Last train didn't come down till four-thirty a.m. so had a little sleep, and in half an hour am going to work again. Some Canadians are beginning to come in now. However, it hasn't been Canada that supplied us with patients, but Anzacs. Last night Princess Victoria's concert party came. I was able to get relieved for an hour to go to it. I couldn't help thinking how you would have felt the extraordinary contrast — pretty, well-dressed girls — flowers — music — and all around tired-out staff and hundreds upon hundreds of patients all fresh from the front line.

The thing that interested me as much as anything — you'd never guess — in the morning I had your letter where a paragraph or two dwelt on the new fashions. It may seem curious, but we never see any well-dressed women — or rather I should say fashionably-dressed women. It's curious that, in a town like Boulogne; but the French are taking this war in desperate earnest.

In appearance they are chic and neat, very, but not fashionable — if the women's pages in the magazines are anything to go by. However, the majority seem to me to wear that large mourning veil you may have noticed in war pictures. Therefore this party, just after having your letter, was interesting as a side line for that reason. I love pretty clothes. The Americans' skirts were to me — remember I haven't been in London or anywhere for months — something of a shock. To be frank, I don't like short skirts as they wear 'em now at all. I think they aren't even pretty.

A point which would have brought the war home to you — right in the middle of the show, an officer got on the stage and said, — "Will all men here marked Blighty return to their wards at once and prepare to leave."

Much joshing occurred, as the men, bandaged here, there, and everywhere, straggled out, — the big joke being to tell those on crutches to double up.

23 July, '16. (Sunday afternoon)

My ownest Lallie, —

. . . . Yesterday afternoon I was moving what we horribly call stiffs into the ambulances which take them to the morgue downtown — where they are buried in a cemetery here, French on one side of the road, English on the other — men with white crosses, officers brown — men three in a grave, officers one. Each coffin is numbered in case relatives wish to claim the body after the war. I detest the job; it seems to me most pitiful: these poor things pinned in a white sheet with a label round their neck, with name and particulars on. A while ago this was a man—a man whom somebody who does not even know he is dead is thinking of, talking of. It always makes me think what awful fools we are to detest one another, and to do nasty things and to say nasty things, when we shall all so soon be just like that. I believe it would be a good thing if, when we contemplate meanness, we could be shown a dead body. It seems so silly—such "bad business "—not to get all the good out of life, when the thing is so short and particularly when we know for a positive fact that we shall all soon be just a lump of lifeless stuff of no account any more. Isn't it funny we don't realize death more ? Gee, but you and I have jolly few things to kick at! I thought that ever so strong, when I was tucking the Union Jack around those fellows.

I don't think I was meant to be a soldier.

12 August, '16.

The heat is fearful, a close, clammy kind of heat, and my work entails funny hours: from 6 A.M. to 6. P.M. with breaks in between just at inconvenient times for writing. . . .

You asked about Biggs. He went downtown,

the other day, and never came back. English and French police searched for a deserter, or a dead body in the sea. In about a week, when every one had quite given up hope, he calmly writes from up the line, if you please, that he met some boys from Vancouver going up to reinforce a battalion in the trenches, and he joined them and is at present in the front line. Can you beat it? The colonel is raving, and now comes the interesting point of military law: can a man desert *into* the trenches? What looked like a tragedy has developed into a huge farce. No one has ever heard of a similar case. The only point is that, if nothing is done about him, others will be doing it. It would be an awful joke if he got a Blighty one and came here as a patient *en route;* wouldn't it?

A coincidence—have just put into an ambulance, *en route* for Blighty, a pair of twins—joined together—wounded together—here in same ward together—and now gone away together.

I daresay you know—have heard frequently—that the army is the one original place for wild rumours. I have always refrained from telling you any before; but I'll break a rule tonight. You know the R.A.M.C. has moved all the fit men from hospital work and are using P.B. or permanent base men, the fit men being sent on more strenuous work up the line. We have heard repeatedly that the C.A.M.C. was going to do the same, but so far nothing has been done. I was talking to our O.C. to-day. He told me that all fit men were being taken from here. What that means in detail I don't know—but I wouldn't want you to hear suddenly that we had all been moved up the line. It is quite possible that all of us who are able will be put to work at more general usefulness—which is sound common sense, as you will be bound to agree. You will hear of course immediately I know anything definite.

Did I tell you we had formed an orchestra here? It is developing finely, every one says. The boys pay half the cost of the instruments, and after the war they have them. Last night they played for a couple of hours, and I could hardly believe they were all learners, a month or so ago.

What must be the general make-up of a person's mind, who collects, packs and mails all the way from Canada a parcel of "literature" for the boys in France—consisting of *Literary Digests* dated 1912? I see some one has done it here. Queer, eh?

This story is *true*. When a man dies, his effects are sent to his parents. A boy died here, his simple things were sent home. An indignant letter came back to this effect,—

"I gave my boy. You have had him—

why steal his things? Where are the pair of gloves and the tin of zinc ointment I sent him?"

Monday.

.... Our speculations about Biggsy and what was to become of him were settled the other day by his arriving in the charge of a couple of military police. I saw him in our little "coop" — which is a wee room, probably some old monk's private room, 'way up under the tiles. He just looked fine and was all enthusiasm. I got about the first intelligent "fresh" description of the line I've had. It appears when he went downtown, he met a couple of friends, and possibly over a few drinks (though Biggsy does not overdo it at any time) the three of them must have imagined themselves back in the States and decided to beat it to the front line. Only any one who has been in France will realize the absolute, colossal impudence of such an adventure; and, maybe for this very reason, it succeeded. Not once in ten million times could it have come off; but it did this time. Not a motor truck, not a wagon can move a mile without being inspected, even down here; and every yard you approach the firing line, things get stricter. Nevertheless, by climbing on a rock train and hiding in the rocks, they made it. When they got to the reserve trenches, they enquired for the particular battalion where

Biggsy had friends, and eventually found it, calmly marched up to the Major's dugout (he was a pal of Biggsy's) and told their story. They were sick of the base, couldn't get transferred to a fighting unit, so just came up, and there they were ! Biggs says the Major couldn't quite grasp it, couldn't seem to get the thing at all, and no wonder! However, he fed 'em, put 'em under open arrest, and near became a casualty through laughing. They were given duty—till the escort arrived. The things Biggsy told us would make a rattling good short story—but there is no space here to tell you much. One thing made me laugh : he was determined to have a look "over the top", if it killed him:—and it nearly did. Fritz didn't understand his peculiar case, and a sniper nearly finished the whole thing. The main thing that impressed him were the rats.

It appears they positively refuse to get out of the way—just march about the trenches, stop, turn round and look at you. They are everywhere. His trench was under shell fire all the time—He says it's great!!!! When the escort came, they brought him back another way, so he has really seen more places and towns than a fellow would who went up legitimately.

At his trial, he was charged with so many days' absence, and he's now languishing—or rather working more than particularly hard— doing fourteen days' field punishment No. 1. . . .

Next day.

There is more than a rumour that this particular hospital is to move to England. It appears our doctors have long been annoyed that they cannot see the result of their treatment and operations, as no sooner a man arrives than he is shipped to England — or back up the line, if he is soon well enough. I imagine that their wishes carry some weight, and there doesn't seem much doubt the Unit will be moved this fall.

Now I haven't the slightest wish in the world to go to England. I am sick of this, I'll admit; but only in that I am sick of a base hospital, so I have tried to engineer a transfer to No. 1 Casualty Clearing Station. They are located at Bailleul, which you see on your map is a few miles back of the trenches. It will be more interesting — more *real* work.

This is a good unit, one of the best in France; but — I don't much fancy life in England. I'd feel all the time I'd be better at home, or in France, anywhere but Home Service.

I don't know, of course, if I shall be able to make the transfer. It's the hardest thing in the world to do, for some reason; every obstacle is put in a man's way. But I think I may make it, and I really hope I do.

Don't be silly and think, because Bailleul looks on the map as if it were "right up", it is. It's located like this, and protected by hills. Naturally such a large clearing station (or rather stations, as I understand that they have recently made arrangements to accommodate the enormous number of one hundred thousand wounded) would not be in danger of shell fire.

It has another good feature: the Clearing Station Units will go home before the General and Stationary Hosps. — and, even if it were only five minutes sooner, it would be worth it.

A fellow came in, last night, with a fractured leg. He came down with a busted aeroplane from a height of two thousand feet. The officer was killed. It seems a tall story: but it was particularly marked on his "wound card" and the Royal Flying Corps would not make the statement, if it were not true. . . .

I have got another green envelope. My very much delayed inoculation positively takes place tomorrow night, without fail, and as the dose is bigger'n ever this time, no doubt I shall be a sick woman the following day, and not even in the humour to write to the dearest one in the world.

Evening, Friday, 25 August, '16.

It's raining and one can feel autumn coming on. The nights are pretty cool, and darker earlier. A month today, it's your birthday. Maybe I'll be up at Bailleul — I hear they have aeroplane fights there every day. It's a headquarters for some sort of 'planes, and as soon as Fritz comes sailing into view, up whirls one of ours and a scrap ensues. Must be a great sight, eh? I've seen lots of German aeroplanes and watched the shooting at them by the French anti-aircraft guns. It's exciting, but I guess the other is more so.

Last night, they put the lights out about nine P.M. A Zepp. was over the sea; but, as she headed for England, they switched 'em on again in about half an hour. Doesn't it seem remarkable how they follow them along, and time them to a second ? The wonder is more are not brought down. The war news today is nothing startling.

Thursday (evening).

Today is the day we receive the wounded from these first big counter attacks Fritz is making — and there are not a few. Guess I've got an all-night session ahead. I took one fellow to a ward, who had been buried two days and blown out again by a shell. He says Fritz is surrendering very freely because they are going to make one tremendous counter attack and get back all the lost ground. This wonderful act is going to take place in about seven days, I hear, and evidently one or two of 'em have heard the slogan "safety first" (Oh, by the way, you may not have heard it, yet, though) and decided our English prison camp looks good to 'em. Don't blame 'em.

Later.

Did you read of Fritz shelling the hospital at Bethune ? It's quite true; a lot of doctors went from here to take the places of those killed. One fellow who was wounded is here. A shell actually dropped in an operating room, and killed doctors, Sisters and patients.

Altogether Fritz is fighting very "dirty" just now — *very*. All are agreed on that. All those tales you read about their dugouts are true. They have electric lights and everything, and have undoubtedly figured on their line being impregnable. However, it isn't, by a long way. All the boys are agreed that the Germans, taken on the average, will not stand up when it comes to a show-down; though they are tremendously clever with artillery and have unlimited ammunition and machine guns.

I see you got a letter from little B——— . He says we had good times together? Well, I'm glad he enjoyed 'em. I never saw him after he left the hospital, and I rather think his times with the girls are imaginary, as I heard he went up the line almost immediately. As a matter of fact, girls in France don't have much to do with the English soldiers. It would be hard for you to realize, living where you can go where you like, do what you like, etc., that neither the French people nor we can do anything or go anywhere without permission. For instance, there are no autos other than military, and a few taxis. You can't go for a walk or a drive—civilians or military. Every few streets has its barrier with the sign "*Arrete*" and two French soldiers with fixed bayonets. Every one must have a pass to go anywhere. You can't take a room, or go to an hotel, without the Secret Service are on you right away, and require your complete history. You cannot enter France at all, without all kinds of passports—but harder again is it to get out. There is no such thing as a man or woman taking a trip to a near-by town, or going on a holiday, or anything like that. Everything gives place to the war, and the French, to my mind, have this business of running a town under military law to a science. You cannot stand a moment on a bridge, you must be off the streets at 8.30 p.m. The docks and all stores and so forth are surrounded with barbed wire and French and English police with revolvers or fixed bayonets, and the place is alive with plain clothes secret service men. Active service is ruthless, and there is no consideration.

7 September, '16. (Sunday Evening)

. . . It is a fearful day, just pouring down with rain, tons of it, in true European autumn style. It was the same all last night, and I guess will be the same till about next July. It will be terrible, if it's the same all up the line—and I guess it is. Also I suppose it will cause a halt in the "move." I wonder if you at all realize what an amazing, wonderful thing this move is, realize that the Germans with all their so-called thoroughness and their thorough understanding of war according to their own rules made by themselves, having for eighteen months prepared a position, we have gone and walked right over it—manufactured machinery and trained the men to do it. Remember not one mistake has been made, not one. Have you ever thought, supposing all our carefully thought-out plans, our reliance on the morale of our new troops: any one tiny thing had gone wrong, all the world today would be saying that we were gone coons; that we could not beat the Germans at their own game; that the sooner we quit and got the best peace terms we could, the better. Instead, not one thing has gone wrong. Our amateur soldiers have proved as good as trained men, brought up to breathe the very idea of a victorious war. Our machinery has stunned the enemy. All the German ideas of artillery have been outdone. In the air we have absolute supremacy, our men even coming down to fire on troops with their machine guns. Only the other day, one came down to engage an anti-aircraft battery that was bothering him—surely the height of cool courage. Now we have invented a "land battleship"; I have spoken to a boy who was near one that went into action; he said all the Germans in the mine crater it advanced on, threw their rifles in a heap and stuck up their hands.

All this is being done without any "frightfulness." There are signs that Germany is "getting wise." And when she does, we may hear of some inside news that might hasten the end. We do not know yet what kind of a loser the German is en masse, but I have a hunch he will not make a good one.

But to return to the beginning as I said: supposing just one calculation of ours had gone wrong, we would all be feeling it differently today. It annoys me when I think people are taking it all for granted; it sounds kind of "German." We are super-men, sort of; we can imagine people saying,—"Of course, I always knew we should win." What rot! No one knew we should win. No one knows how near we may have been to losing at various times, and now to take it all in that self-satisfied, I-told-you-so way, is—well—horrid.

The boys who come down hourly don't say "I told you so"; they know beating Fritz is no cinch. They say he is outclassed, is getting weak. They know we are winning, because—we have worked for it; our soldiers are men, not machines. They know we are better led, our artillery is superior—in a word we are better men than Fritz. Moreover, our cause is the right one.

Later—and I don't know what I intended to say in that sentence.

However I haven't much time. You will understand that. The boys up the line don't take prisoners by the several hundred and reinforce concrete machine gun emplacements without more than a few getting put out of mess for a while, and the greater the activity up there, the more we are kept busy down here.

I was with you in spirit on your birthday, all day, and at night my head was on your little cushion, and your photographs were underneath it—yours and the young You, our Bill.

Never, never get low-spirited, down-and-outed. You won't, I know. It's only a mood when you are, and passes in a day. We have no reason, either you or I, to be down-hearted. We cannot claim this war as a reason—else half the world would be. Yet, what else have we to complain of? Are we not well and fit ? Have we not all we could wish to build on, the will to do it, and the brains ? All is well with our world. . . .

In you, I have all I need—all I want.

Dearie Lal—Good night.

III
UP THE LINE

III

UP THE LINE

My very dearest Lal, —

The last letter I wrote was the green envelope one, two or three days ago. We have been particularly busy one way and another; one thing, we have moved from the convent into billets in small cottages. It's very funny; there's a long row of cottages by the coal mine, just cheap, rather sordid-looking places all exactly alike, same as the rows of small houses you see in England. Each has a small back room on the ground floor just eight feet by twelve feet in which ten men live somehow. The people who live in the rest of the house you never see, as they lock the connecting door. One backyard for each company is used as a cook house, and at meal times you file over with your mess tin. Of course, some houses are better than others, cleaner; and maybe one is lucky enough to get the French people to boil coffee in the morning and odd things like that, but those places are very rare. Mostly

87

all the people are phlegmatically indifferent, and don't seem to take any interest in their own lines, any more than any one else. It's rather a good thing we are so closely packed, as, the floor being brick and the places fearfully draughty, you have a better chance of keeping warm at night. The weather is awful; dull, heavy skies, rain most of the time, and mud. We'd be wet all the time, but we got an old can, punched holes in it, and have made a brazier for the room. It's remarkable what a difference a little fire makes.

The other night, we went on a working party up close to the lines. You wear your tin hat on these expeditions, and go at night. After you've walked six miles or more, the latter part with a shovel and maybe a pick as well, you feel as though you had enough, even before you start the night's work. On the way, we passed through a fairsized village, every single house which I saw being shattered, the church in the square just having the four walls standing. Of course wrecked villages have become monotonous; but when you see one first, the desolation and waste of it all strikes you very forcibly. A thing I noticed particularly was that, at a cross road where all the corner houses were smashed flat, a little wayside shrine, like you see in every village, with its large crucifix was absolutely untouched. I hear this is very common all along the line. Curious, isn't it? When we arrived this far, the flare lights sent up by Fritz and ourselves were very bright, and looked only about a block away; but of course they were much more. These are sent up continually all along the line, playing in the air over "No Man's Land" for a few seconds, lighting up everything very distinctly. Quite a little firework display; but you don't think of it that way.

Our work was digging a narrow trench to put a water pipe into the front line. They have had it all along; but recently the frost froze it up, so the engineers wanted it buried a couple of feet. We all strung out and were given twenty feet apiece to dig. I guess you would have thought it rather weird, digging away there in the dark, in the distance machine guns tapping away exactly like woodpeckers. They loose off a few rounds every few minutes on roads, and where they think there might be working, or ration parties like ours ; also now and then you hear the sharper crack of a solitary rifle — a sniper at work; but you hardly notice these things. You are too busy with your bit of work and getting home again. By the time you have done the return march you feel as though you had done a pretty good night's job, the march being by far the hardest part.

Sunday (evening).

This morning we were out on the range. I did fairly well at rapid firing, but rotten at the other part where you take your time. Later, we were at the bombing school — live bombs, now, of course. This evening we get paid — fifteen francs. Hardly a fortune, is it ? But enough to buy two decent feeds, anyway. While on that subject, I cannot impress on you too forcibly the importance of parcels, regularly and often. Down at Boulogne, a parcel of eats didn't amount to much; but up here they are just Godsends, absolutely. Down there, if you wanted anything nice you could get almost anything from a Sister or an orderly, but here the rations are the same every day, and awfully monotonous; cheese, jam, stew — that's all. And lots of hard work all the time. Most boys get parcels very often indeed, and naturally your own crowd all share up alike. Last night, one of us got a cake, chocolate, *café au lait*, etc., and sitting round the old brazier we were quite happy for a time. Even if you had a lot of money, you couldn't buy much, not in a small village like this. There are Y's, of course; but they are too far away, when you come in late at night and tired. . . . By the way, will you find out if there are any books on the subject of trench first-aid? It will have to be some that were written since the war of course. The first-aid books generally sold are no good for up the line, as they don't take account of conditions under which the work has to be done. If you find anything that you think may be of use, I should like to have it.

Let me know that you are happy and well. Remember, always, I am *yours*.

—Battalion Canadians B.E.F.
France, 13 November, '16.

My very dearest Laly —

This morning we arrived at our destination behind the hues. We didn't do anything but loaf around today after we arrived, and tonight I discovered this Y. about two kilometres from our billets, so I could write to you. First, dear, you will be glad to hear I am particularly well — couldn't be better. Things seem to improve all round as the days go by. We are billeted in a school, have two blankets — quite ample — each, and the grub is first rate. Havre is like a bad dream already. The train journey also improved. There was more room after each change, and the weather is lovely. Boulogne, on looking back on it, seems more of a slothful existence every day; no contrast could be greater than the life there and here. Of course no fit man, not having special training for particular work necessitating his staying at the base, has any right there at all, in my opinion. This is most certainly *my* place.

All along in the journey, I tried to collect impressions to give you, and I cannot help but smile when I think what they were. . . . On the whole trip, I don't think I ever heard the war mentioned. There was a poker game at each end of the box car which seemed to be the greatest attraction. The conversation was mostly kicking on the room, the grub, the army in general — every one in the army kicks all the time. As we approached the line, the guns became audible and I am half ashamed to say I felt a thrill. No one else even mentioned them. Even right here in what is, in manner of speaking, only a stone's throw from the firing line, life is more peaceful than in Boulogne. Kids play in the streets ; the shops are lighted up — dimly — but still lit; this afternoon I heard "school" going on in part of the building in which we are billeted. The only difference I can see in the traffic — to that of the base — is that the A.S.C. drivers have a steel helmet strapped somewhere near the seat. . . .

I shall anxiously await every letter from you — I am so worried as to how you will bear up — you positively *must not worry,* dear, a lot. You know in the first place how it upsets your health and again you must be brave for Billie and me. She must not see you not being brave — and I want always to think of you with your head up, taking whatever is God's will, like the brave woman I know you so well to be.

What deep satisfaction will be ours, when this war is won, that we *both* did all we could. . . .

My heart and mind are with you always, dear—literally always—more now than ever do we understand and appreciate our great love.

Never be downhearted — never gloomy — God must be on our country's side.

Kiss our Billie many, many times for me.

17 November, '16.

My dearest Lallie: —

Today has been bitterly cold — roads all frozen hard, almost like Canada. It must be the very devil in the trenches. I remember it was rotten last February; but then it was mostly wet, slushy snow, not hard, dry cold like this. We are somewhere between Arras and Bethune. Late this afternoon, I went with some of the boys for a long hike to see if we could see "something." We jumped an auto truck and went several kilometres in that. We wanted to get closer up the lines; but we didn't make it and all we saw was a bunch of aeroplanes being shelled with shrapnel. We came back in an old French farm wagon. Every village and hamlet — quiet old-world places, two years ago — is now full of troops, wagons, water carts, and all the paraphernalia of war. All seems to work like clock work. Every one seems just to have his own job and be doing it cheerfully without fuss — Wherever you look on every side road are lines of big auto trucks, and in and out go fast motor cars and auto bikes carry ing the despatch riders. The roads are in splendid condition, kept so by Fritzies — who seem perfectly happy and contented. Each one carries a mess tin like ours, and over his shoulder a gas helmet. Even the kids in the street carry them. In places, too, are gongs marked "gas alarm" in case it should come over. At all cross roads, everywhere, is a sentry to direct traffic, etc. The organization seems perfect, and everywhere you breathe the utmost confidence in the very air.

During our walk we dropped in on the 6th Field Ambulance boys — that is, the Ambulance attached to our Brigade, the 6th. They are billeted in a whacking great French chateau. In peace time, no doubt, it was a beautiful home. The conservatory is now the men's mess, and leading from that, in what I imagine must have been the drawing room, a room all panelled in marble, are rows of stretchers on old packing cases. It's a ward where the 6th boys look after sick cases. Two of the stretchers were occupied by Fritzies — both of them all smiles. One said he had been just six days from leaving home to getting captured. They said they were tickled to death to be out of it.

Field Ambulances are divided into companies or sections and take turns going into the trenches. These boys go in next week again. Of course they live and have everything much better than we do; it has always seemed peculiar to me that

the infantry, who after all really win the war —
have to take all the dirty end of everything —
grub — billets — every darn thing. And, after it's
all over, the boys who go home behind the brass
band will be all these base and staff boys; the
fellows who won the war will mostly be pushing
daisies right here in France. . . . This district
hasn't been shelled much — Adjoining us is a coal
mine; a shell has taken the big chimney half
off — a darn good shot, if it wasn't a fluke, — but
the mine is doing business night and day as
usual; you can see three or four of these mines
round about and all are going full blast.

18 November, '16.

Today broke bitterly cold — real Canuck
weather with some snow. Luckily we have those
sleeveless leather coats which turn the wind fine.

Another fellow and I thought we would like
to find the 29th layout this a.m. Weil, we walked
I bet ten miles over hill and dale. Once we hit a
village which had been all shelled to pieces. The
big chateau was uninhabited and looked most
desolate, all broken pieces, with the bell rope
at the big entrance gates hanging swinging in
the wind, and holes in the roof, the lovely
gardens all weeds — a lovely place utterly ruined.
Eventually we found the boys camped in a little
wood. It was the first camp of its kind I had

seen, and the first impression I had was a lumber camp—long, low, brown bunk houses, cook houses, almost exactly the same. The bunk houses are built with earth floor, on either side rows of rather flimsy bunks. Wire netting forms the mattress. At either end were a couple of braziers going. They were very dark—most every bunk had a candle stuck on the side. The boys were all as cheerful as a bunch could be. They say it is regular home after the Somme. They were out of the trenches two days, only sustaining two casualties, those being two reinforcements whose curiosity made them want to look over the top.

28 November, '16.

My very dearest Lal:—

I have just got a parcel from you—a box of cigarettes—and they could hardly have come at a better time. As it happened, I didn't have a blessed thing left to smoke, and was wondering what I was going to do, when the fellow came around with the parcels. Thank you ever so much, dear.

I guess you will notice that my letters now are rather hasty and all unconnected. Try to bear it always in mind—because I guess they will get worse, if anything—there is no place to write at all in the billets, no tables, chairs, or anything like that. You eat out of your mess tin, sitting on the floor. There is a Y.; but it's too far off to go often, and moreover you get pretty tired by night. Last night, I wrote you, as usual, on my knee—on the floor. All my letters are written under difficulties, and to have a mind at peace and in mood for writing is out of the question. Last night, it appears, Fritz either put an extra heavy shell over, or exploded a mine or something. Anyhow, the boys in our room say they woke to the sound of windows breaking and the ground shaking; but I was so beastly tired, I slept peacefully on and never heard a sound. Always heavy on the sleep stunt; remember?

Evening.

A heavy fog came up before we quit work this afternoon and it turned wretchedly cold, so I am going to turn in early, hoping to get warm that way. There was very little mail tonight. It worries me so to know, as I do, that you are worrying, and the worst of it is I cannot write—talk, we used to call it—as I want to. The thoughts are there, but the expression—the way to put them on paper, simply won't come. I don't suppose they will ever come, until this is all over. I know how you will miss it too—but I am happy in the knowledge that we are in such complete accord that you will realize—everything. The things we discussed and planned and debated over must now lie over indefinitely. It is quite impossible, under these conditions, to give much thought to anything but the barest facts of just living, eating, sleeping, working. But the intellectual side of life, the beautiful things, the clever things, you simply never think of them. The reason I am mentioning this at all is I want you always to try and see things as they must be with me, and judge accordingly. Letters have meant more to us than most; haven't they ? I suppose I will get most terribly out of touch with things, with the live, progressive world we both so love, and books, and what is really happening in "our" world; but again that cannot be helped, either. You must keep pace with things for both of us, and "put me wise" when I get home.

Good night, dear, I'm going to bed, God bless you.   **R.**

Next night.

I think I told you that the Batt'n I am momentarily attached to is made up of fellows just out from England and casualties returned from hospital. They belong to all kinds of Batt'ns but are all in the 2nd Division. Just now, things are quiet up the line, so our own crowds don't keep wanting re-inforcements. As they do want them, they take them from here. We are known as the 2nd Entrenching Batt'n; but there are no trenches to be dug, so we do fatigue, and a little drill etc., also bombing, and musketry — that chiefly for the fellows fresh out, who have been trained with the Ross, which of course is not used. . . .

I can recommend Northcliffe's book just out; *At the War,* I believe it is. You must read it; it will surely be good. To my mind, he is one of the greatest Englishmen, but many would disagree. He is very outspoken, and English people seem to loathe anything like that. . . .

In France — behind the lines.
Sunday afternoon. 4 December, '16.

My very dearest Lal, —

I have got hold of a green envelope, probably the last I'll get for a long, long time. They don't issue them here; I got it by luck and good management! Do you remember the letters you wrote, when you thought I was going up to a Casualty Clearing Station? You were worried about it being dangerous, when most of them are safer than England. If you worried then, what will you be doing now? And how can I say, "Oh, that'll be all right." I might — should — say that to any one else; but what's the use of talking a lot of hot air like that to you ? On the other hand, what's the use of dwelling on the black side of things? This war is so "different." In any other we might talk of "our noble cause", "the clash of arms", "death or glory", and all that kind of thing; but this one is so vast, one wee atom of a man so small, the chance for individuality coming out so remote, that it has developed, for a single Unit, into merely a job of work to be done: eat, sleep, and work. You don't fight; you can't call dodging shells, machine-gun bullets, and bombs, fighting; it's fighting all right, when you "go over"; but a single battalion doesn't go over so very often, even at the Somme. I wish I could make you "get" the atmosphere. "Heroics" are dead here, a charge is not the wonderful, glorious thing we were told it was. I have even begun to wonder if it ever was, or if the poets and historians and "Press agents" of those days have been just kidding us.

No one wants to go into the trenches, yet no one (who is any one) would dodge out of it. Every one wants a soft Blighty wound, with the chance of getting to where there are no whizz bangs, and you go to bed every night. Every man I have spoken to: German, French, English, Canuck, are sick to death of it; yet to quit without a definite decision is out of the question, and no one would think of it. And how on earth am I to tell you not to worry and all that; how on earth is a husband (like me) to write to a wife (like you) about his feelings on and before going into the front line of a war like this.'^ None of us are heroes. To read of "Our splendid Canadians" makes us ill. We are just fed up, longing for the end, but seldom mentioning it, and hoping — when we think of it — that when we do get it, — it will be an easy one, or something final. Our main effort is to think and talk as little of the war as possible. The mail is far the most important thing; the next, "What's the rations today?"; the next, "What's the job today.?". Of course newspapers are anxiously bought up — but we know the newspapers don't tell us much. And the thing is so big anyway that no one can possibly grasp even a fraction of it.

There is one new thing I've learned, and that is that it won't be good to be a chap who stayed at home, when the boys return. This thing is just a bit too serious. We know what it is here. Also, the distance between the fellow at the base and the fellow in a fighting unit is "as a great gulf fixed" — far, far more so than the innocent boys at the base dream of. Again, as you know, the later Battalions formed in Canada don't remain as a unit, but are drafted as reinforcements to older ones, N.C.O.'s of course reverting to privates. Well, I don't think I should like to have to say I belonged to the one hundred- or two hundred- and- umpty something. The question always is —"Why.?" "Out of a job"—or "Did the girls make you join.?" How long have you been in France is what matters. . . .

I'm not sure if you would like me to talk about

how I feel regarding the possibility that I might "get it good", as they say; — but, dearie, I don't think about it. I did a lot at first, but don't now. Thinking about it could do no good; in fact, I fancy a man couldn't do his best, if he perpetually had that thought in his mind. As regards your future, in case I got killed, well, I have thought that all out; but I am not going to say anything about it — mainly because you are so much better than any man could hope to be — a higher type, dearie, altogether. It is much too sacred a thing for me to "talk" of, sitting on the floor of a barrack room, surrounded by poker players, all sorts of people, — I couldn't.

Regarding the kiddie in that event, my views on her future so exactly coincide with yours, that there is nothing left to say. I have told you before that I consider you a perfect Mother, — more I cannot say. Billie will be in perfect hands; she will have a Mother such as I should choose if I had the whole world to pick from.

14 December, '16.

My dearest Lal: —

I have had a jolly interesting letter from you. I wish I could write the way you do — I mean in a chatty way; but I can't. I seem always to be strung up to an unnatural kind of pitch, never have a mind at complete ease, and the consequence is my letters all seem to me to be forced and not a bit like I want them to be. But I know how you always want something regularly to tell you I am well, so I will send as many of those cards — the boys have named them "whizz bangs" for some reason — I mean, of course, the post cards. They are not exactly interesting; but they will show you that I am still up and going strong. Today, I have been reading about the German peace proposals. My impression is it is very clever of them; but, of course, we shall "carry on" just the same. I think that every horror that has so far been enacted in the war will be outdone in 1917, and that the German common people will not stand another winter, and so it will end. But not, in my opinion, with an out-and-out knockout either way, or with any huge gains of territory by us.

Things are still exceedingly quiet on this front, which I am directly behind; in fact, you could hardly tell there was a war on. . . .

By the way, has it ever struck you what a force, politically, the returned soldiers will be after the war? Lord Northcliffe has drawn attention to the fact that, after the Civil War in America, the men who had fought, controlled the country for fifty years. I suppose those cocksure politicians would smile, if you told them; but I prophesy that the boys out here will run things, when they return. You see if I am not right. You will see they will hang together as one man. It will be the greatest "frat" in the country . . . .

18 December, '16.

My dearest Lal:

Just a very short note. We are moving billets, hence the hurry.

I was highly amused to hear the tanks are made in America. Germany also claims originating them. No, dear, let poor old England have something. They were designed and built in a town in the North of England which I know well. And, by the way, don't get the impression they are the whole cheese; they wouldn't be worth a nickel without the human element — the infantry. However, soon I will see one work, enter one, and will give you my impression (with one eye on the censor, of course).

About the war — and me — there isn't much to be said. Things are still delightfully quiet. It snowed today, and tonight it's beastly cold. The new billets, I think, will be an improvement. Hope so.

I haven't been out on a working party for a few days, and am anxiously hoping one won't come my way till Xmas is over — but I have fears.

Most people, I think, imagine, when you are at the front, you spend all your time in a trench, looking out for Heinie. My last few days have been spent digging holes to bury old cans in, and hauling flags for the floor of a large tent. Nothing very warlike or romantic about that, is there? But all these little things have to be done, you know, and about a million of them.

26 December, '16.

My Dearest Lal:

Xmas has come and gone. It was horrible weather, rained all day, and a gale of wind blew so hard even walking was difficult. As far as was possible we had a good time; I cashed the P.O. the day before Xmas eve—there were four of us to share it and it lasted till this evening. We didn't have any parade Xmas day, so we spent it visiting various friends in different billets. I had just moved to mine, the new one; it's a sort of washhouse back of a cottage, just room for three—about six feet square. We have a little stove and the woman in the cottage, being a little more civilized than the general run, we can use her coal pails to wash in and so forth. There was no Xmas dinner, such as the papers say all the troops get. The issue was the regular tea at noon—with the addition of prunes. At night, the usual "Mulligan", or stew. However it didn't make much difference to us, as we ate in the village. Just as we got to bed, Xmas Eve, all the surrounding batteries started a big strafe and continued till twelve o'clock sharp, as a sort of Xmas box to Fritz, I guess. It made such a row and shook the place so we couldn't sleep. One big gun throwing heavies over sounded just like the street cars approaching, as you wait often, no doubt, at the corner of Second Avenue; the light in the sky was exactly like summer lightning as you have seen it flickering scores of times.

Today is very clear and, as I write, Fritz is very busy shelling our planes which are up in great strength, I have never seen him hit one yet.

I think they are getting a bit more lively on this bit of front. You remember my telling you about that ruined village I was in one night? For some reason, Fritz took it into his head, the other day, to put a few more shells into it, and one fell on four of our boys who were cooking their grub. It was rotten luck; but they never knew what hit 'em, I suppose. Also—probably you didn't—but you might have seen something like this in the papers: "In the Arras section, we made a raid, capturing fifty odd prisoners." This was when four hundred of our boys went over the top here the other night. It was a very successful raid. They stayed in Fritz's line an hour and a half, and only lost a few killed.

The other day, they asked for volunteers to take machine gun corps instruction. I thought it all over very carefully, as I would rather like to be a machine gunner—but I finally turned it down. I want to get a job as Battn. Stretcher bearer. It's a rotten job, of course, and nobody wants it; but I rather think I would be more use binding up wounds than I would be just carrying a gun in the ordinary way. I got quite a little experience in the ward at Boulogne, which will be a lot of help. Moreover, I think it's interesting — much more so than merely being in the line.

During the big wind the other day, our Y.M. tent blew down, and I was unluckily on the party working at night to fold it up — so we have no place to go to write or anything. It was a new institution for us; we have only had it about a week or so. As the wind tore it very badly, I guess we'll have to go without one now.

Several batteries have started another strafe and the window of my little shack is rattling to beat the band. The big heavy, I think, is a new addition; it certainly sends over some pretty husky shells, very much to Fritz's annoyance. I suppose the planes have been sending down some fresh ranges this morning and that will be the reason of the extra bombardment. The old woman in the back yard goes on calmly with her washing, merely remarking to me "Bon for the Allemagne." Nothing seems to excite those old people now; they have seen so much of it. The thing that surprised me, and what I can never understand, is why Fritz doesn't shell this town. He must know we are here; his planes manage to get over every now and then. Also all within a mile of each other are three or four coal mines, all going full blast. I should imagine he'd go to great trouble to put 'em out of business. Also, he never makes any attempt to bring down our observation balloons which, on a day like today, are up all along the line. On this sector, we simply have him beat to a standstill in every department.

If only he'd get worse and quit; but no such luck for another year, I'm afraid.

My little house looks very cosy tonight. I'm all alone. We got a little table, swiped an old chair, the stove is going fine, and I've just made a mess tin full of tea (strong). Later, I'll manage some toast. We are well stocked with Oxo, cakes, *café au lait*, and a plum pudding, also some canned butter. Somebody rustled up some shelves which are decorated with home photographs. It doesn't look much like active service in France, until you notice the other war decorations: gas helmets, rifles and so forth. Did I tell you I was through the gas school — tear-gas. You go and stay in a big dark shed full of it. Rather weird it is. It's to test out the helmets. It smells of pineapples; the gas Fritz uses is more dangerous as it's colourless — I dread that — and being buried — more than anything.

Anyway, one may go through Ypres and the

Somme, say, and never get a scratch, and another get hit by a bit of our own aeroplane shells miles behind the line — so I don't suppose where I personally go matters much. It's written — and what is to be will be, and only time will show.

30 December, '16.

My very dearest Lal, —

I always thought Friday was my lucky day; but I guess I made a mistake and it is Saturday; because, in addition to have an easy day, I got two letters and a parcel.

Tonight our little shack is decidedly cosy. Bill is lying on the floor on my blankets, reading a magazine he swiped: the stove is red hot; we have had a big feed of hot "mulligan" topped off with what we both think honestly is the very best cake we have ever tasted. We have good cigarettes, and I have a new pipe. Later on, we will have some hot Oxo and some more cake, and the weather and Fritz can go hang till tomorrow. The parcel was the Xmas one. It was lovely, the packing the most thoughtful I have ever seen. Everything has a use out here. The tin is what we wanted to keep our jam and cheese wrapped in; the stickers make a nice wall decoration; string — we always need string. So you can see that all of it comes in for something. You don't know what a "parcel" means — you couldn't. It's the nice feeling you have when they come, apart from the eats which seem almost a necessity, and the other things which are of the utmost use.

I see you say some one told you that any parcels going to the hospitals would be kept there and disposed of by the boys in the care-free way they have. That is only half right. They wouldn't down there; but they would up at the Battalion, and really it is only right. The fellow may be dead, or in Blighty or some place where he won't need it. Some one, some place, is no doubt shaving with my Gillett's blades, and some one else has my other presents — but, *Que voulez vous?* The only thing to do is to register small stuff, and sew everything else up *most* carefully. Too much attention cannot be given to packing. No one would think of redirecting a broken package. What would be the use?

I was ever so pleased that you wrote in such a cheerful strain. I know it isn't all put on. And you want always to bear in mind that an awful lot of the stuff you hear about the trenches is a great deal exaggerated. It isn't as bad as all that, and anyway a Battalion isn't "in" all the time, you know. Some of the boys will even be "out" for a whole month. Those boys, that you get in conversation back there, try to give you all the horrors and none of the fun of it.

31 December, '16.
Sunday — (New Year's Eve).

My very dearest Lal, —

Today we were quite lucky. Apparently there were no parties to go out anywhere, so we went to Church in the Cinema Hall. It wasn't very interesting. Tonight there is a special service — with communion, if you wish — it is a voluntary affair — at seven-thirty. Chaplains who know how to talk and interest men up near, and at the front line, are awfully scarce. I've only heard one real, live, sincere one, and he was at La Havre. . . .

Did I tell you at Xmas the boys who drive the big transport trucks all decorated them with holly, and the big gun fellows actually hung mistletoe on the guns ?

That's one reason why we can't lose the war: our boys are irrepressible, in a sporting way, not surlily savage. That spirit wouldn't last. Ours will. Only the newspapers talk of Huns. They are always Fritzes to us. The boys kill 'em with the same good nature that they laugh at them, when they come in as prisoners. The most common remark is, "Hello Fritz! When's the war going to end?" Fritz soon catches the spirit, and goes about his work quite cheerfully. He has a canteen of his own, and can smoke and all that. His rations, I think, are identical; I know he gets a third of a loaf of bread, just as we do. It wasn't him that invented gas and Hquid flame.

Mention of gas reminds me Arras was shelled heavily again the other day with gas shells. My chum Billy was gassed slightly at the salient. He and others were asleep, when he thought his rubber sheet smelt funny—Fritz was shelling all around; but nothing special. Suddenly he thought perhaps they were gas shells,—and kicked up as many sleepers as he could, meantime trying to pull his mask over his head—(that was before we got the fine new ones) but he hadn't time. It was beating him, so he stuffed as much of the thing into his mouth as he could and beat it. A great many died. He's a fine husky lad; but he's never been the same, he says. His eyes are not so good, and his chest is bad now and then. He was wounded too, and wears a little gold stripe; also he's a corporal. I'll want you to meet him some day—

I am getting more impressed every day with the perfect organization and readiness of things here. Whatever it was before, today I cannot see a fault, not one. Of course, we all kick all the time, "grouse" as the English call it; but that is a soldier's privilege. We kick at the rations, the work, everything; but that doesn't signify anything. If we shouldn't win, it is not the soldiers'—by that I mean the Armies'—

fault. Everything is like a perfect, well-oiled piece of machinery. All the men are well clothed, good boots—so essential. All the men are well; there is no sickness whatever. I mean no fevers and that sort of thing. All things like tools for every purpose are here in abundance; ammunition—well—in more than abundance. Our planes are up in the sky all the time in flocks, and the big guns—I don't know what to say about them. I don't even begin to know where they are; but I know wherever we are, one is liable to make you jump by letting off a round or so, apparently out of the earth. The transports run day and night with the regularity of trains; and reinforcements of all these things are right here, right at hand. But most of all, the right spirit is here. Every one knows we are winning. There is no fuss—no hurry. The vast organization is like a successful business, running smoothly with plenty of work and orders on hand. I wonder if Fritz can say the same. All I know, his batteries do not reply to ours, his planes put a show in once in a while; but, in less than two minutes, he is surrounded by little clouds of bursting shrapnel and our flying boys are after him like a hawk on a pigeon. He never waits, always turns tail and beats it. Also, I think he flies too high for accurate observation. Truth to tell, I don't blame him.

All this speaks to only one end. Only a silly ass thinks we are going to pour through, and on to the Rhine. This isn't a war of pitched battles of that kind. Moral effect—that now common phrase—matters more and more, and will be the decisive factor—Army—then Civil. To advance a mile doesn't sound much; but imagine what it would be if Fritz advanced a mile here! It isn't the trenches; but the vast organization behind that suffers most; the roads and routes, the cables, the 'phones, the billets, gun emplacements, supply depots, and Oh—everything. To put that out of gear is what counts.

Behind every mile of trenches is literally a town—a temporary town, true; but a town with all its organization from water supply to electric light. Say, what a fortune a fellow could make —will make, many of them—conducting' touring parties through here, after it is all over! Then millions will come; I'll never rest till I come here myself. I want to see the Salient, Courcelette (Our Capture), and I want to see Fritz's side of the thing. I suppose all the dugouts and trenches will be left for generations for this very purpose; and old French farmers will coin money out of otherwise barren land. Souvenir hunting will be interesting; queer things will be dug up—unless the French Government prohibit touring parties until all is made sanitary—which I guess they will.

Wednesday, 3 January, '17.

My dearest Lal: —

Yesterday, I was working just in front of one of our batteries, helping build a railroad track. Our batteries were giving Fritz no rest, all along the line. x\t dusk, you could see the flashes from many guns too far away to hear the report. Not a single shot did Fritz push over in return; in fact, it's hard to imagine that there are German lines "over there." In the morning we had to squat down and keep still for a while, as two Fritz planes were up. But they didn't come far. In addition to a barrage put up by our anti-aircraft guns, more with — or at least much with — the idea of heading him as bringing him down, were a number of our planes quite ready for him, if he came too far. It must all be very discouraging for poor Fritz; but the worst is yet to come no doubt, in the grand finale. Everything is going.

I was rather amused (forgive me) at your idea of my possibly getting "cut out", over the top, and about the ration "sewn up in your coat."

My dear, a Battn. doesn't go over the top once to a blue moon; moreover, going over, the worst thing you suffer in a trench — holding a crater for instance, is far worse. And you don't have anything sewn in your coat. I don't worry a bit about my teeth; but I do about my eyes,

which are getting very poor indeed, especially at
night. . . .

5 January, '17.

My Ownest Lal: —

Mail is beginning to come with regularity,
and I am tickled to death, of course. I keep
getting some from the Hospital, which is out of
date to say the least; but most of it is right bang
news, cheery and optimistic, breathing of hope
and above all telling me you and Billikins both
are, as we say here, "Jake" — in other words, fine.
Those are the kind of letters I love to have, and I
feel better for having read 'em right away.

Today all sorts of "domestic" happenings
seem to be around our little home. To begin
with, our orderly Cpl. has gone up the line on a
draft, and B. has got his job. That makes our
room the Post Office, nice for getting your mail
tout suit, but a nuisance, somewhat, owing to so
many callers. W. marches in, this afternoon,
with the green slip which is more precious than
rubies, the most valued thing a soldier ever gets
in France — a leave ticket — for ten days they are
now, too. His mother is over from New York on a
trip to London. He's been here twenty-three
months in France without a day's leave, and
maybe he isn't tickled. (It almost looks as if I
might get mine after all.) The shack is all in a
flurry with him packing up. You have to go

with full kit, minus ammunition. It's a darn shame we should have to wait so long, when base fellows, and officers, can go over so often; but of course the Infantry, indeed, any of us up the line, take all the dirt of everything, from grub to work.

And now you may wonder how I happen to be *'at home" in the afternoon. Well, a fellow out on a working party fell to pieces and went insane. They took him to the field Hospital, and I am one of his guards till they've finished "observing" him (I hope it takes six months). They, of course, consider the possibility that he may be pulling one big "swinging the lead" stunt; some darned queer things have been done here to get back to Blighty or Canada. I do twenty-four hours, and same off, with another fellow; it's a cinch. The Fid. Amb. is, at least the headquarters are, in rather a nice chateau — what's left of it. I told you about it once before. The jay is in one of the rooms upstairs which has been turned into a ward and by a coincidence is presided over by a Med. Student, one time of No. 3 down at Boulogne. It's a fine big room with three large long French windows overlooking the grounds; the wall paper is modern and rather pretty; the beds consist of stretchers on low trestles; there are, of course, none of the refinements of a base hospital, no sheets or anything like that; if any one is wounded in the trenches, he goes to the advanced dressing station. . . .

I was going on, when some one remarked "That must be one of Fritz's." No one bothered to get up to look out of the window even. Later, a fellow casually remarked that "Fritz had put a few here this morning and one had dropped on the coal pile near the billets." Not the slightest interest is taken. Remarkable, isn't it?

I am sometimes amused when you mention the fellows who you know in khaki and things about the two hundred-and-umpty something battalion. The first thing those fellows think about when they get as far up as this is to get rid of those nice pretty badges, and pick up the ones of the battalion they reinforce. We think they took their patriotism rather late, you know; don't you? Certainly, I never want any fit man of military age, who didn't go to France during this time, to come near our home; and I guess he won't — twice — !

Your remark about the returned men being somewhat "difficile" is exactly what I expected — and it will get worse. There are two sides to the question of the boys, in my idea. One is that they don't want a lot of fussy people patronizing them. All they want is what is coming to them and to be left alone. The other is, of course, that a very large number will undoubtedly trade on the fact that they went to France for their country's sake — whether they did or did not they'll think they did, and try to bum around till doomsday. What it will be like when all return, I don't know; but I expect, if any one thinks they are going to mother him in a patronizing way, they'll be dead out of luck, and will of course blame the poor Tommy for what is due to their own lack of tact. There are going to be some rude awakenings on both sides, I guess. The English people take the thing better and more sensibly, because they all realize it more, have given more and lost more.

The Returned Soldiers' Association sounds alright. But, as you say, it will have to be free of all interference. Personally, I don't give a hang for anything of that kind. All I want is to get to Canada, and they can keep all that's coming to me. I'll gladly say I never was even over here. All I want is to get there — and to be home with you. . . .

Of course, S. wanted to come to France. Personally, now that I have been up here and seen what it's like, I don't see any reason for fearing anything should happen to him beyond the ordinary risks. He would not be intrusted with a 'phone or wire job on the front line, but would be given some base, or advance base job, practically bomb proof. Certainly it would be ten thousand times better for him in every way to be up here than in Shorncliffe. You are kept busy here. The work is taken more or less seriously, which it certainly is not at Shorncliffe. The wildest forms of amusement are sitting in a French estaminet drinking their wine — quite harmless — or so-called English beer — more harmless still — in the company of the old woman inn keeper and her family. Women are taboo, I suppose by the French Military authorities. Whichever way you figure it, this would be the best place for him. Moreover, I don't see why he shouldn't take his chance with the rest. I thought differently about it at Havre, I know; but I've changed my mind.

However, I don't suppose he'll be allowed to come. Two kids out of our battalion were sent back, as too young to fight, recently. The humour of the thing lies in the fact that both wore gold wound stripes got at the Somme — kind of late to decide that they were unfit. But the boys worried a lot, you can bet; they were just tickled to death.

When I think of how quiet things were here when we first came, and the situation now, it makes me — wonder. Of course, there was always a bombardment — of sorts. But not the kind that keeps the light flickering in the sky at night, *all* the time; nor did any of the guns let out a roar which shook the ground. Now — well — things are altering. . . .

Fritz came over in one of his "planes", the

other night, and dropped a few—He must be getting quite bold again.

Every fine night, our planes go over to drop bombs on his billet, and picture shows, etc. Next day, weather permitting, they calmly go over and take a photograph of the damage. Our air service is simply magnificent and must undoubtedly be a great discouragement to poor Heinie. We took his punishment for two years; new it is his turn. You'll notice I don't say much about going "down there" now. I think our business will be elsewhere. Also, I think we Canadians as usual will be right there—probably for the Anzacs to get the glory. To get the true light on them, you have to ask an Imperial's opinion. He gives it in no uncertain words—"*no bon.*" Every town in England swarms with them on leave, where our fellows cannot get it on a bet. Out here, taking your objective is easy; holding, after Fritz loosens up his artillery, is what counts. History will show. We took and held; Australia took alright, but did not hold. ...

A thing I forgot to mention amongst the things I would like you to put in your parcels are candles—the thick kind, if possible. Whether in billets or tents or dugouts, you don't get them— at least we don't—issued, and there is no other light. The French shops charge twopence halfpenny each for only a small one, and a dollar fifty a week doesn't go far enough. In the line.

the boys get an old jam tin, cut up a candle in small pieces; put a layer on the bottom, then a piece of sand-bag, then another layer of candle, and so on as far as it will go; and you have a thing which you can fry bacon or boil a mess tin on. Some stove, eh? But quite effective.

You ask me if the socks you sent were jake. You bet they were; but too good. Very common—very thick ones are the only thing, so that you can throw them away. Weight is all that matters in your kit. My shaving kit, a comb, a few pairs of socks (most important of all), photographs and letters, two pipes, a pencil and cigarette case are all I own in the world. I am busting with health—glad to be here in every way, far more contented than at Boulogne—and sure of victory. *Positive* of it, this year.

Next Day.

My nice soft job has gone back on me. The guy was proved "dippy", and the fellow who was guarding while I was off has taken him down the line.

There is no doubt the fellow is crazy. He thought he was going to be shot for cowardice. I think he was afraid of being afraid, till it got him—only a young fellow. The first night I was with him, he bothered me all the time to let him go out and dig his grave. It's not uncommon for fellows to go crazy in the front line. . . .

Today I watched miles—literally—of guns and men on the move. In Canada or England, it would draw people from a hundred miles to see; but here it's so matter of course that even the French civilians don't bother to turn their heads. The thing that impressed me most was that the men went about it all just as they would in ordinary every-day life. The gun drivers just went on like ordinary teamsters—and so on, all down the line. The whole thing is just a job of work. You get so used to the thing that nothing whatever seems to surprise you. . . .

11 January, '17.

My Ownest Lal,—

Both mail and parcels come regularly now, though of course many letters have gone astray, particularly those you must have sent immediately after I left Boulogne. It's too bad. I wanted them particularly, but though I now know your views, my mind is more at ease. I depend so much on you and value your opinion so highly. Yes, I got the parcel. The cap will be most useful, particularly on night working parties. The steel helmet is rather heavy and clumsy, and you will have seen in photographs that the boys almost always wear something of this sort under it. We get a thing issued; but it's a cheap affair, and not much good. I'll have to cut holes at the sides for my ears. You need to keep them uncovered. The socks are fine, but still too good. I want cheap ones, also only send one pair at a time.

Who told you "Imperial" tobacco was good? Good! I'd always sooner have tobacco than cigarettes. We get an issue; but it's not always regular, nor good.

The steel mirror was particularly appropriate and welcome. Of course they are the only kind. I have one already, but it's a small one and had lost a lot of its polish; they do in the damp and wet. Glass ones are no good at all, as your pack is your seat in the day time and your pillow at night. Gloves we get issued. Maybe they last a week, at most; and you have an awful time getting another pair. My issued ones were all holes, so yours came just at the right moment. The best kind are those strong Canadian leather ones that workmen wear in Canada and the States. In England or France, there is nothing like them. When you are on barbed wire work, you get the loan of a pair of specially made canvas things. Excellent they are; but you have to turn them in again, when the job is done. The boys try to swipe 'em, but are not often successful.

Your letters are different now. They mean more to me. Of course, they are not the same letters you wrote to Boulogne at all. I like them much better. But you always do seem to do the right thing at the right time. I am so afraid you will think mine lacking in heart, but they are not; they were never so full of it, if you can understand. Somehow it's impossible to write of our homey heart-to-heart things. This life is too big. The time may be too short. You are my comrade; my pal; you are here with me in spirit. The small things must wait. I look on you as living through life with me actually. And if you were here, we would not have the time or inclination to talk of the little things which are really the big things. We should mutually agree to let them wait.

You can be assured that, when the time comes, I shall not be behind in keeping up the standard you would wish. It is your standard that I shall be acting up to, the one you set. Whatever happens, you must always remember that you are *with me* every minute; that it will be more you than me that will do the things I do, that I shall always think first — What would Lai do? — and do it.

The whole division is moving — not "in", but "out." We shall have a "rest." (Good word that — The Army must laugh in its sleeve when they call it that. When the division is out for a rest, it's the hardest time they have: drills, parades — endless fatigues.)

I am great friends now with the Madame who owns our wash-house home. Sometimes she asks

B. and me In for a cup of coffee, and we give her part of our parcels for the pickaninnies, as they call the children here. Across the street is an old, old woman who I call my *grandmère*. She calls me "Poppa", and comes in to see us sometimes. She is a great old scout, wears the familiar sabots. She has a face like an old, old apple. A man who is married for some reason stands ace high with her. When you go to see her, you must sit with her and be right at home. B. is the *gentil Caporal* to her; she likes him, too. She has a high, shrill voice you can hear three blocks away; and a heart of gold. When the old French Madames are good, they are very, very good; but when they are bad, they are just shrews. Of course, there are no men, only those who work in the mines, and some very old men. In one sector of the front, the French lost seventy thousand men in one battle, in the early days of the war; but we shall regain that ground, this year, and much more. We have the guns now.

To give you an insight into the "every dayness" the "so-used-to-it" feeling of things held by the civilians here : the other day, old Madame's niece, who is married and whose husband is in the "Transhays", came home at noon, an unusual thing. She works in a laundry. B. says, "Hello, a holiday today, eh?" or words to that effect.

The girl says, quite unmoved, "But no, Monsieur. The Bosche, he threw over one big *bomm bomm*. It fell in the laundry yard, and the monsieur he say, 'You all go home today.'"

Imagine the concern if the Bosche threw one little high explosive shell into the yard of the laundry at Ottawa!

We are worrying Fritz night and day here now. He is never allowed a rest. The scream of the "big heavies" passing over is with us most all the time, and the little eighteen pounders closer up are always at it. We have him beat, and so careful is he of his ammunition, or disclosing a battery, that he seldom replies. He does sometimes, though. I guess he gets exasperated, and feels he has to.

These are great adventures, *the* great one for many; but they don't get the limelight. We are close enough up to the line for us to see things in our wash house when they are up. A big raid is usually about two hundred men. They creep over with blackened faces, mostly on their tummies, with fixed bayonets, bombers in the lead. Immediately before this comes off, usually for two minutes or so, the artillery puts up a bombardment, the like of which you cannot imagine. This is to clear Fritz's men. If this is not done completely, the boys must come back — some of 'em. These raids serve several purposes. We find out just what Fritz is doing

in the trenches, destroy machine gun emplacements, but, main thing, bring back prisoners.
From them the Intelligence Staff, which by the
way is wonderful, find out what regiments are
*'in", who is holding that particular bit of line,
and many, many other things.

We control No Man's Land from La Bassee to
the Somme—something to say. Fritz's raids are
only a joke; his attacking days are over, anyway.
You will note how almost absurdly confident I
am. I am using my own intelligence ; these ideas
I have not got from others. We are top dog—
every one knows it. Thousands and thousands
will make the great sacrifice, of course. It will not
be easy; but the game's now ours. We only await
the word. We have everything, men, guns,
everything, and the winning spirit. No one is
crazily elated. It's a job of work to be done
calmly and quietly; and it will be done. And then
we'll come home.

Recently our bunch have provided the Prison
Guard—that is, the German prisoners. In the
morning, you go down, stick five rounds in your
magazine, fix your bayonet, and take a couple or
so hundred prisoners out to work. You go in
motor lorries, about forty to a truck and two
guards. The bayonet-fixing is a matter of form
and a joke; one couldn't drive Fritzie to escape
with a club. About seven miles out are some
stone quarries, and they break big stones

into little ones for the road. Taking them in the bunch, they are a poor-looking lot — Somme prisoners chiefly. I was rather interested in the job, as I like to talk to them, hear their point of view, etc. They wear the uniform they were taken in, for the most part. Some wear an old Canadian cap; most wear puttees they have made for themselves out of sandbags. Those with no overcoats carry an English issue rubber sheet, same as ours. All carry gas masks. Guess they know their value. Their food is the same as ours. They work just as little as they can get away with, and laugh and talk and smoke to their heart's content. "For me the war is finished" is their tune.

Part of the day I was on, I was taking small parties of my own to different jobs. On one occasion a man said to me, —

"Are you the man who is taking us to fetch that lumber?"

"*Lumber*!" says I. "I guess you learnt that word in America."

"Sure, I'm from New Haven, Conn."

A good-natured, merry little man, it appeared he was on a trip home to Germany in 1914 when they grabbed him for the army — very much to his disgust. I guess he saw to it he was captured; the Canucks took him at Courcelotte. I asked him about the war. His remarks are unwritable — but — he'd like to see Kaiser Bill in the trenches.

Of course he doesn't work; he is invaluable as an interpreter. He was quite happy, very fat, merry and contented. And—I rather gathered he held his "Kamerads" in contempt; he was "American."

Others I talked to, who had a little English, told me Bapaume and Peronne were untakable ; that the war would finish in three weeks. All agreed that, but for England finding the money, the war would have been over long ago, with victory to the Allemagne. But victory is already theirs—no doubt of it. The little tubby man from New Haven, though, was silent.

Write and tell me of everything—the little things—and often. What Billie says. What you say. What you do. And what you think. Everything. You are my life.

26 January, '17.

My dear Lal:—

I haven't written for a day or two because it has been positively too cold. Sounds rather funny, but it's true. Our billet, which is cosy enough for ordinary weather, has quite fallen down on this Canadian kind. These little outhouse places are not meant to live in, in the first place; but pass alright for ordinary weather. We never noticed till a day ago, for instance, that there are two holes in the roof and several million holes around the walls and floor. We have stopped up all we can, and we look after the stove with more care than you ever did Billie. We just cannot get warm. To make things worse, a draft came in with no blankets, and we had to cash in our extra ones, so now we have only two each. I have never seen weather like this outside Canada. Paris said yesterday was the coldest day on the Western front. Honestly it's the limit. What it's like in the trenches won't bear thinking of. Indeed, I don't know how they stand it at all.

I am tremendously thankful for my more or less easy job. Working parties and parades don't look good to me just now. When at home here, we sit huddled over our portable small stove; when at work, there is not time, and what there is, is spent trying to warm up.

31 January, '17.

My dearest Lal:

Conditions are just the same, only a trifle more so. I'm writing this, sitting almost plumb on top of the wee stove we have, and I am freezing to death, at that. It doesn't even improve when it's bedtime. Two blankets in this are just about as much use as none at all. To give you an idea: last night I don't suppose the stove went out till about twelve, yet at six this morning, a mess tin of water left on it over night was frozen solid.

When I look back on conditions as they were here when I first came, and now, I am very impressed with the change. Every day seems to add something to our already splendid organization. Every now and then we put up a bombardment which must be an eye-opener to Fritz. To give you some comparison to go by, I'm told by one who was there, that last year at Ypres nothing like the amount of shells were put over by us. At that time, of course, Ypres was the most important point of the British line. This point is hardly ever mentioned in the communiques, yet we can now bombard more on an insignificant front than we could last year on the most important. You remember I told you Fritz never retaliates in either shells or planes. That is changed. He is quite frequently over us now; but not in any strength, never more than two planes at once. Also he throws an odd shell over now and then; but nothing to matter, anyway not near our billets.

You don't think that I spend my time picking rats out of my clothes and skipping out of the way of Fritz's shells; do you? Not a blooming shell has fallen within a mile of me as yet. I wish it would; I want to see one bust. I'm far safer than I should be helping you to light the furnace at 77———

I'm worried, too, terribly worried. It's whether my turn for leave will come before it shuts down for good. Believe me that's some worry to pack around. The thing I chiefly long for on leave – or things, I should say – are unlimited hot baths, meals brought to me by somebody else, no reveille, and lots of good shows. Do you realize the fact, when I tell you I haven't been inside a bath for thirteen months, only stood in drafty thin huts under a shower, a very poor substitute indeed. I think you will faintly imagine the luxury of sitting in hot water, with a cigarette and an evening paper. I intend – should luck favour me – to spend considerable of my leave sitting in a bath. And eats! I haven't really had a decent feed for a year. But most, I think is the longing for one short spell away from military discipline. My God, how I hate it!

There is a concert here every Wednesday; but it's held in an old marquee, and the weather doesn't make me feel much like going to 'em. Also, every Saturday, there's a boxing tournament open to the whole division, but I don't go to them for the same reason. I never go to the Y., because it's too far away, and there's nothing there anyway – I mean not a sort of club, like the Boulogne one was. Up here, war is a business, and you have to be on the job. Down at the base, it's a sort of glorified picnic.

I mentioned at the beginning of this about the cold, and spoke of it in the past tense. Tonight again it settled down in a regular Canadian freeze.

I am sitting right on top of the stove, with my candle propped on somebody's parcels beside me. One side is cold, the other twenty-five degrees colder. It's rotten weather. We have lots and lots to strafe it for.

15 February, '17.

My life at present has got into a groove, it would seem, and each day is exactly alike. I have got used to bombardments. Even as I write, Fritz is almost directly above, and our men are trying after him on all sides.

The thaw, I think, has set in for good, and it's more than welcome, though the mud and wet are pretty bad. I got a new pair of boots just in time, the first pair I've ever had in the army, so can keep fairly dry.

Leave is stopped now for some days, and my little vacation seems as far off as ever. I suppose the trouble is in regard to boats. Fritz is sinking a lot of boats, a devil of a lot, and even though it seems so good that the U. S. has broken with Germany and all that, so many ships will not sail, and our supplies must be curtailed. I may be wrong—I hope I am—but I think this is an anxious time for us, and I believe history will show it. However we shall cope with it and overcome it, and that's the main thing.

You will notice that a great many raids are being pulled off just now. A good many are pulled off on our bit of front—any time of night now. All at the same second, a perfect roar starts up—every gun at once. It's rather magnificent while it lasts. Last night it was very dark while I was taking my messages, and the gun flares were most welcome as they lit up the road most opportunely.

17 February, '17.

The time for our battalion to send up a draft has come at last. I suppose I shouldn't write you tonight till I'm sure they won't want me; but I am pretty sure, not on this one. I think, when my name comes up, "not available" will be the order; I hope so anyhow. There's lots of time yet, lots of it.

We are of course interested in this move on the Somme; but no one seems to be enthusiastic because no one seems to quite understand it. The general opinion seems to be that Fritz has something up his sleeve; we seem to be suspicious of "retirements"; we only understand complete annihilation by big gun fire. We hear now and then weird stories of a new and powerful shell, but nothing definite. One thing, however, I can vouch for. I have seen a copy of a German officer's (captured) report to his headquarters, mentioning our using a new and terrible explosive. However, he may have been a green hand and got over-excited. A few days after I saw this, it appeared in the English papers — the copy of the captain's report, I mean. You can guess whether these communiqués are interesting or not. I can't tell you of them, of course; but I may say that we know the names of the company commanders in front of us on each sector of practically every relief; we know what regiments are in front; where they came from last; in what strength they are, and all about them; we know when they commence a new trench or sap, where it runs, when (if) it's finished, and also all about it and many, many other things. How is it done. There you've got me. I dunno'; but I do know it is done, because I see it. If any one says to you we haven't got an Intelligence Staff, you can afford to smile. . . .

18 February, '17.

. . . While on this subject, I'm afraid there are going to be some fierce ructions here and there in Canada, after the boys come home. I read an article the other day on "Slackers — the Army is Watching Them." The fellow who wrote this was an officer and he'd got his ideas from censoring the boys' mail. Every one who writes to a soldier tells him about the slacker who did not go: the girls — his own people — every one, and he writes back and says what he thinks of 'em.

He is too busy, and life is too jolly uncertain, to worry much about it — *now*. But wait, when he is home and feeling safe and good. Do you think he will want to pal in with a chap who stayed safe? I don't think. Do you think he will not rub it in now and then — maybe roughly ? I wonder if the slackers have ever thought of this. If they have — well, I'm sorry for them; their thoughts can't be pleasant.

20 February, '17.

I often think how significant it is — how the world for years and years has covered itself with a sort of armour. Very clever it all was. People with money and no brains, to cover their lack of brains hedged themselves around and called the hedge class distinction, even educated themselves in separate schools, using a different accent and form of speech. What a joke! Then along comes this war — more than a war, that word doesn't describe it — and off has to come the armour, and a man is just a man — or not — as God made him. What surprises, what shocks must have occurred! But you can't realize it as I can, because you have never seen the home life of England as I have.

Right here in our little shack is a splendid example. There's a young Englishman million-aire, an ideal boy at a pink tea, able to talk rot to women by the hour, very careful in his appear ance — *and* quite useless to any one. Along comes the war and dear little F. enlists; he is a duck in his uniform, and holds his own right up till he reaches the front line; *then* — falls all to pieces. Quite helpless — opinion worthless — just ignored. And then B.! Quite useless at a pink tea, would be unnoticed anywhere at home. He runs an electric crane or something for a living, has worked ever since he could walk, nearly. *Here,* where things matter, B. is looked up to, his opinion counts; he wins promotion; an ideal man to live with, a hustler and a man.

Now — when it's over what's going to happen? Do we drift back in the same groove?

I tell you yes, with a slight difference, only — F. again will be the pretty useless doll (only more so as he'll talk F. and war); but only till he gets in company with those who have been and seen. Then he'll beat it, of course. B. will be as before, too. He'll never talk war; but he'll have added a number of staunch friends, friends for life.

And that is my opinion of how it will be. These cases are typical of many thousands of others; it just happens that I live with the two extremes.

Curious.

There doesn't seem to be anything else, just yet, happening between the U. S. and Fritz, but I really think it will be war. Lens has not opened up yet and there are no signs that it will lift. There's a fellow I came up with from Le

Havre due back tonight. I used to knock around with him quite a bit. He was LCpl. here. As he knew something of bombing they made him Sgt. Instructor. He learned on the Somme, by the way. He taught me here. One day while teaching a bunch of recruits, a fellow lost his nerve — they do sometimes — and after pulling out the pin, got scared and dropped the bomb into the next bay where there were three officers and a man. There was just five seconds to act. G. ran around the bay, picked up the bomb and just got it over the parapet in time. . . .

3 March, '17.

My very dear Lal,

The weather still remains most boisterous and stormy, the wind is terribly cold too, and there seems little chance of the wind decreasing any as yet.

I saw something this morning most interesting; a large number of our boys going through an attack as nearly similar to what they will have to contend with as possible. They used flares and worked in conjunction with aeroplanes circling a few feet above. The planes signalled, "Morse code", I think, with motor horns. It was most realistic. Signalling the lifting of the barrage was rather amusing. Two men with white flags advanced ahead, and were supposed to represent it. Hardly looked the real thing. Any thought of a home manœuvre or sham battle, though, must be quickly dispelled, when you remember that in a very short while it will be done again through a hell of real fire.

(I wondered last night if I am taking too many liberties with green envelopes. In Orders were four battalions who had lost the privilege through one man being indiscreet. The name of the individual one was published. I think I'd sooner be shot than have my battalion lose through me, — I guess I would be, anyway, — I must be very careful.)

In bed — most uncomfortable !!!!

The runner who goes for the mail returned with some awful news, tonight — awful! The 29th want twenty more men on Tuesday, and I don't think there are twenty men here, so — your uncle will have to *partee* (French for beat it). B. sent me the news with a message that a pal of ours had volunteered to go as he had not got cold feet. I'm sending him a message that he has to go, too. I've been making a cover for my Gillette tonight out of waterproof silk usually used on wounds — also one for my diary (for I keep a diary now) in anticipation.

Personally I think I'm lucky to have got the worst of the winter over in positive luxury.

I hate (and fear) cold and wet; but when the sun shines and it's warm, I'm awful brave, ready to eat up all the Fritzes in France.

I particularly hope they make me a stretcher bearer; but they may not. There's no honour in the damn job, and no chance of advancement, or anything but work. But I like the work and I understand it a little, while I hate looking after a beastly gun and forming fours and all that. If I'm not a stretcher bearer, I shall try my best to be a bomber or a gunner — something you can specialize on.

17th of Ireland, '17.

My very dearest Kid: —

A few days ago, I was sent out as stretcher bearer to a party going up to work farther up the line. I was tickled to death, as this place, after five months, is getting monotonous. We marched off in the afternoon with full kit: two blankets, tin hat of course, and all, and believe me I was thankful I didn't have a rifle to carry nor ammunition, only a few medical supplies, — just bandages and dressings, and a bottle of iodine in case of bad accidents. There is always a field ambulance somewhere near.

Well — we eventually arrived and found our billets, in huts like I have told you of, and like the pictures you have seen of the Y.M. huts. Inside are rows of bunks three high, with chicken wire as a mattress. Anyway that night, hearing the 29th were near, I set out to find them, which I did after a long hunt, in a village. There I met B.

and all the others I knew, and stayed the night, borrowing an overcoat and blanket to sleep in. I half wish I'd come for good. They seem a great crowd.

I have always been under the impression that it was busy back where we were; but up there was a surprise. No word of mine could begin to describe it — even if I were allowed. It's terrific — absolutely unbelievable. Miles and miles in endless procession of munitions and men.

Wait while she opens up — and you'll hear all about it.

Next day, I went out with my party, who were to keep a railroad track which runs right into the support trenches, — a positive cinch for me — nothing to do at all. One fellow cut himself with the shovel. Another fellow had a sore heel, And another fellow had to go with the field ambulance ; he had the grippe, and they kept him there. That was all I had in the few days.

Next night, the Corporal in charge and myself took over a tent and moved in with the party rations. It was about a foot deep in mud and water; but you get used to that, and with a kit bag, which I used sleeping bag fashion, and several sandbags I slept fine. Read awhile — "The American Prisoner" by Phillpotts—by the light of two candles stuck on my tin hat at the head of my bed in the mud. It was altogether much cosier than in the hut, more private, and nicer everyway. The Corporal wasn't a bad fellow, either, and we got on well.

I can't tell you exactly when I'll go up; but about any time, I think. I am quite ready; the days are warmer, though the nights are still cold. I am anxious to go; the sight up there got me all excited. To be out of it is to be out of everything worth while. I would not miss the beginning for anything. . . .

One of the boys tells me it is awfully dark and hard to find your way in the trenches at night. I guess this will be rather rotten for me, because my eyes are none too good at night.

I am thinking about you and storing up things to tell you about all the time, though I won't be able to tell you anything yet awhile.

I never do or see anything that you do not share with me in spirit.

Good-bye for a day or so, Lal dearest.

18 March, '17.

Things are still going jolly fine. You have read often about the cages we put the German prisoners in. Well, I have been busy this two days helping make one of barbed wire. It's some way from here and we go over in auto trucks. Today it was fine but beastly cold; I nearly froze. Yesterday, when we were working, who should go by but two of my very old tent mates from No. 3, who had left later than we and gone to another outfit camped near here. We may see something of them, as they are attached to the 2nd Div. too. . . .

We passed two observation balloons yesterday. You have seen pictures of them; they look big enough to fly away with the engine affair which holds them down by what looked to me a terribly thin cable. Aeroplanes, of course, are over all the time — *ours*. I haven't seen any of Fritz's yet. The guns are going most of the time. At night, you can hear the machine guns, too. Everything is all most casual and "every day alike." Last night we went for an evening stroll. A Frenchman, passing, said,

"Masshin — Masshin pop-pop-pop — No bon-no bon — No — no bon, M'sieur." — referring to a machine gun in the distance.

I mention this to give you an idea of a passing salutation of the evening "out here." You would probably say "it's a fair night." Both remarks would have the same enthusiasm or spirit. "It's an awful war," to quote a popular phrase.

Harold Chapin in his letters said he had heard more genuine laughter out here than anywhere else in his life—I guess he was right too—human nature is queer.

21 March, '17.

My Ownest Lal: —

I am writing this on my knee by an old oil can which has been made into a stove in one of the familiar huts away down along the line—for again I have been sent out as S.B. for a working party.

This morning, I got my orders to come and relieve a man who has been out here some time. So I packed up my belongings, few as they are, and set out on my hike. I hadn't much to carry, the steel helmet and gas mask being the heaviest items, I guess. I got a loaf of bread, a tin of jam, a can of beans and some cocoa, so I wouldn't starve. It was a cold day and snowing a bit. Shortly, however, I hit a stalled motor lorry, and got a lift a good part of the way. I soon found the party's billets in a hut right next the Y.M., and found the other S.B. He had fixed things up for himself some, had a little table affair with a real drawer, and had collected a good stock of medicine from the adjacent field ambulance. His bed looked real cosy in the middle tier of bunks. I took it all over from him, and have now settled down. He has just gone and supper will soon be here—and the boys in. It looks like a fine job, if it lasts.

I act as M.O. absolutely, and am responsible. In this case, I don't go out with the work party, but stay in the hut. Sick parade is at seven, when I see which men should go in the field ambulance and see the doctor. Any man who gets hurt out on the work they send for me. The rest—the cough medicines, binding up cuts, and so forth—I do here at night.

Next day.

Went to bed early. My predecessor certainly left things jake. He has four blankets and a rubber coat. At the head of the bed, he'd rigged up an old biscuit tin which makes a swell candle stand. It was as cosy as could be (you will note I still turn in early to read).

Sometime during the night, I was wakened up by a battalion coming in to sleep in spare bunks. They had just come out of the trenches — been in ten days — and were coming out for a ten days' rest. They had no blankets, and it was snowing hard outside; but I never heard a kick. Guess they were too glad to be "out."

The last time I saw this well-known battalion was on review at Shorncliffe. I remember how well they looked, every kilt swinging in line. I'd like you to see a battalion come out fresh from the line. You wouldn't believe it. • The Scotch cap had given place to the steel helmet and the kilts to trousers and puttees — what you could see of 'em for mud. Though they only arrived about one or two a.m., their Field Kitchen at seven A.M. had hot tea, bacon and bread, and jam and cheese for them, so good is the system, and it never breaks down. . . .

The only thing I fear is the weather, the wet, the cold, the long nights and the mud — not the shells, though I guess I'll fear them enough later.

And every day spent here means nearer the warmer weather. . . .

You will be tremendously impressed with the big retreat—many seem to think it very smart of Fritz making us begin all over again; but I think it is not thoroughly understood. *It is a retreat*—that's the main thing.

Understand writing is always most difficult now. Sitting on gasoline tins round a wee brazier made out of an oil can—it's almost impossible, but I'll do my best.

22 March, '17.

My dearest Lal:

Yesterday I went back to work on another of those "cage" things I was telling you about, a small one this time—cosy, two huts and everything fine—too fine in my opinion.

I am getting quite an expert at the wire entanglement business, and if any Fritz can get through the path I made, he'll have to go some. In the evening, I had a most interesting conversation with Fritz. I rather hated to do it. He was wearing the Iron Cross Ribbon which he had won twice, and I couldn't help thinking of the numbers of our men he must have killed to win it. I asked him if he had got it for killing Canadians. He was most pitifully emphatic in trying to convince me he had only been up against the French (of course). But what got me was his total inability to grasp the fact that this war could last over this Christmas, with a victory for Germany, of course. He told me it was a total and complete impossibility to take Bapaume. He was quite serious. He considers the war as won. So it is! I cannot understand it. If the German soldiers think like that, how can you blame the civilians ? It would seem to me that any intelligent man, — and many of their prisoners seem very intelligent—could not help reading the signs, even from the narrow confines of a prison camp. Every man they see has victory written all over him. They couldn't look up in the air at any time of the day, without seeing one of our aircraft coming or going in perfect peace. Our observation balloons are plain to see, all day. No one molests them. It would seem to me that this gross ignorance of the real condition is going to prolong the war more than anything else. . . .

29 March, '17.

I didn't finish my letter last night, I was too cold. This morning is the wildest day we've had for a month, a tremendous wind, and rain and cold. There certainly won't be many planes up today; they couldn't last a second.

The other night, after I had finished writing you and was just off to sleep, all of a sudden what sounded like all the guns in the world opened up at once, and sleep was out of the question. I always wish, when I hear or see anything so magnificent, so powerful as that, that you could be with me for a while. Here is like having a front seat out of danger. I read somewhere that to imagine a modern bombardment, you must think of the greatest thunderstorm you have heard and then compare it with a little boy beating a drum; and I guess that's about right. Myself, I never can help thinking of all the ground and stuff being churned up, where the shells are all bursting. It's undoubtedly awe-inspiring and magnificent. It's unimagineable how anything could possibly live in the face of it. We all thought that the big strafe had begun; but evidently it wasn't so.

I think that Fritz will have his hands full to hold the Arras-Cambrae-St. Quentin line, and I believe he thinks that the time we shall take coming up and attacking him can be utilized by him on another front, say the Russian front.

But I believe we intend to fool him. I think we are going to drive him on this front, beyond anything that has happened on the so-called Somme front.

We may even take Lens and Lille; we may do anything.

One thing I can assure you of positively; that the Somme front is not to be the only one where we shall have big battles.

Whether we can win this year or not, I cannot think.

America coming in, which now seems certain, is bound to make a difference; but all our efforts might be cancelled, at least in part, if Austria had big successes in Italy, or Russia could not make good.

Chances of revolution in Germany seem to me to be too remote to entertain seriously. There is no doubt in my mind that Canada is going to take a larger part in this coming battle. It is really up to us. We didn't take the worst end at the Somme, last year; the Australians are there again, as you will know, so I guess we cannot kick.

We'll hope it won't be so bad. I hear it on an eye witness's authority that a gun in this scrap will only have to play on four yards of Fritz's front.

Life is just living. I mean eating and sleeping and "getting by"—if you understand. Meals are eaten standing up; an old gasoline can as a seat by the stove is a lucky grab off, as there's such a crowd. For instance, bunks are in three tiers. That means nine men in a space about four feet broad. You eat off your mess tin, and wade through the mud to the cookhouse for your grub. As a matter of fact, I am now just an animal, a tiny unit for use in this vast scheme, or a tiny bit of machinery, to be kept alive—only just alive and useful at the least possible expense and room. That of course is war; I thoroughly understand it. It's quite alright, and the proper thing. I have no kick. But I want you to grasp all that, so you can understand my letters. The trenches are full of mud and water, and my life by comparison is positive luxury.

The rations are not so bad. I'll tell you what we get exactly. In the morning, about a pint of tea — (good and strong as a rule) either beans — (two to a can) or a rasher of bacon. At dinner, a spoonful of jam, and a hunk of cheese and tea. Supper, tea again — and stew, or mulligan as the army calls it, and the twenty-four hours' bread ration, usually a third of a loaf. Sometimes there is an extra, though seldom; a kind of date paste; one day there were oranges. But of course by the time they get as far up as this, the various "cease fire" outfits they have passed through only leave enough for a ration of three men to one orange, which is what we got. It doesn't sound very remarkable, but it's enough to keep you fit; it does me anyway. In the line, the bread mostly has to give way to biscuits; but when "out" eats are again good. A parcel is naturally an event of great importance.

I have been given another party again today, making three in all. I have to handle all the sick reports for each party, and fix up all the trivial cuts and bruises, and medicines. In addition, there are various parties without any "Croix Rouge" man attached, such as Isolated Machine Gun Companies and odd parties from heavy batteries, who are wise to my being here, Of course

I fix up any of them who come, am very glad to. I like the work; it interests me. It is, too, undoubtedly necessary work, and I must say I prefer work which seems to be real — and worthwhile.

1 April, 1917.

As I said previously, I have changed my job. A chance came along to get into the Medical Hut or dressing station of the Battalion. I took it, partly because I want the practical experience, more in medicine of which I know nothing; and partly it is of course a little superior job. The one thing I didn't like was leaving B. and the old shack, though of course I see him several times a day. My new home is altogether better, only two of us in a larger room with electric lights and stove, with a regular mine of coal from the Q, M. stores. I sleep on a stretcher on a couple of boxes which makes a very fair bed. My new companion I don't know very well as yet. The work is continuous, though of course not hard. I help the others and the M. O. on morning sick parade, which is sometimes very heavy. We're busy through the day with civilian population. Surprising to you I guess it will be that we attend them; but we do, the whole town. They call through the day, others leave messages for us to call at their homes. There are more of these cases than there are soldiers. We get everything from bad cases to little seven-year-old kids who cut their fingers (I dressed a little boy's hand this morning—a wee cut—but I put it in a sling and he is a hero). Of course, all this is free of charge. Bad cases we take all day amongst the troops. The regular sick parade is in the morning. At night—at six p.m. we do dressing again.

We cook our own rations, which are very ample, in the sick room, a house just across from where I sleep, and we eat and sleep more like civilized people than like soldiers, which is some blessing. The hours are long, from about six-thirty till nine or ten p.m. I like it. Of course it may not last long—maybe a month, maybe six months; you cannot tell. They may need us in the hue any time. In cases where the patient is very bad, we send him to the field ambulance which is usually in some chateau or school. If he is only temporarily bad, they keep him until he is well, then return him to us; if bad enough for base hospital, they ship him to the dressing station down the line, and so on.

Our pay is delayed this time for some reason. I haven't had the price of a paper, even, for over a week—the boys down here are just the same.

Our guns brought a Fritz down here this a.m., with the assistance of some of our planes which drove him this way.

And now I must quit. Supper is to get ready, and then the evening parade of sick.

Give Dad's love to little Billie. And best love to you.

IV

IN THE TRENCHES

IV

IN THE TRENCHES

2 April, '17 (morning).

The weather has taken a turn for the worse, most bitterly cold and the ground covered with snow again. Snow over mud, ugh !!! Imagine it, if you can. Under these conditions, thank the Lord I am well — most tremendously so.

All my kit is packed, on the expectation of having half an hour's warning.

All is good.

A tin hat, a gas mask, a razor, a towel, a tube of medicated vaseline (swiped) for my boots, a knife, fork, and spoon. That's about all. Your woolly hat is worth its weight in ten dollar bills. It isn't quite the same colour as it was, but I'd sooner lose anything than that.

Even at this, my kit feels heavy enough.

The snow drove a plane down just now. He was not hurt and flew up again, when the storm blew over. It must be desperately cold for them and the observation balloon men.

I'm getting quite a lot of work now; lots of men seem to be going sick. Nothing serious, but

still sick—boils, and so on. My last party
consisted of French Canadians; only a few can
speak English. It's funny. You'd laugh to hear
me, " Take those two mit now—and this one
après midi—and again *ce soir*."

The horses are standing this weather very
badly. At least ten are shot every morning and
thrown into an old disused trench. . . .

4 April, '17.

My dearest Lal, —

Yesterday I was out to see my old friends
where I had been working, and where I wrote
you from. While there the runner came in and
said there was a small draft of soldiers going up
to the 29th. There are plenty of men here now, as
a big truck came up from the base a couple of
days ago.

On the way home—it was a glorious spring
evening—I came to the conclusion that I
couldn't wait to be put on a draft, but put myself
on. It seems to me that this business of dodging
drafts is getting overdone—I mean by the men
who have never been up. When a man has been
up and come back recovered from wounds, I
don't blame him a bit for trying to dodge going
up till some of the new bunch have had to go. So
when I reached town, I went and saw B. who is
making up the draft. He had the list full, but
took a man off and put me on.

So now, you know. On Sat. — "I parti pour la tranchay," and I feel all excited.

I am busy sewing holes in my trousers, putting buttons on, and so on. I have very little to pack, but I have lots of odd wants in the way of equipment to get, my rifle to get in condition again, and all that. We have an O.C. inspection at ten A.M. Sat., and then off we go. I feel awfully well, and as keen as mustard.

I don't know what you will think of my decision ; but I hope you will approve. It is much better to go than wait to be sent, when it looks as if you had been hanging back.

Just before Easter. Evening.

I am finishing this off in bed. It's impossible to sit up in bed, or my head hits the next bunk; but I'm managing rather well, have got three candles on my tin hat and my pack makes a fair desk. It's quite warm in here tonight. We captured an extra big oil drum today, and have made a swell stove. It's just at the end of my bunk; the pipe runs out through a door. Every thing is very primitive. I'm living right down to brass tacks now. My kit consists of only the very barest necessities: two pairs of socks, no change of shirt. Even at that, it's enough to look after, and pack away at a second's notice. As things are here now, kit is very plentiful, as fellows just leave everything behind when they move. I wear your woolen hat, a pair of high rubber boots (worth about twenty bucks this weather) and long rubber cape. When I go, I'll just leave it behind.

A 29th Sgt. friend of mine, has just pulled in with another working party, and tells me I have to be "the doc." to their party too. That's alright. I like it. I'm "the doc." to everybody. As a matter of fact I am more conscientious and go to ten times more trouble under these conditions than I would if I had some one over me.

I hear again that our battalion is away over strength, so I guess, if I'm lucky, I'll miss the first big battle, which will be the hardest of course. You may or may not know that Imperials took the brunt of the Somme. When the Canadians got there, it was more open fighting, though God knows it was bad enough.

This time, unless I am mistaken, the Canucks are going to open the game; but it's going to be very, very different from the Somme in many ways. All the way back here, the ground is marked out with tapes and flags, arranged according to our pictures exactly as Fritz has his trenches in front of the particular battalion which will take that section. So, if the officers get killed, the men know just what to do. The battalions have been made familiar with them. I have been over some of them; they seem very complicated. Fritz must know what's coming.

As far as I can see, we don't give a damn whether he knows or not. White tents are dotted in the fields all over here, and he's up in the air all the time. Last year, too, the green envelopes were cut out — remember? Not this year, though; I got an issue yesterday.

We are going to give him a tremendous licking right here, I am absolutely sure of it; every tiniest detail is perfect. The men are splendid — no sick.

The battalions even shine up their brass work now, and are all over strength.

The guns and supplies are beyond anything ever known before in any battle in the world. The food is plentiful and good.

Confidence is absolutely the limit — Every one is laughing and cheery as a lot of kids.

You must try and understand now that it is harder for me to write even scrappy stuff like this, than great long letters before. We must leave psychological questions till this is over now. I cannot bother to figure on things like what *may* happen after I get home.

Please send parcels regularly, little ones and frequent. Socks, a shirt (we never get a bath now, there is nowhere to bathe), cake (no candy), a towel, soap, a can of *café au lait*, half a pound of butter, if you think it would keep. . . .

And now I must quit. My shoulder is about dislocated, and my left arm is asleep. The man in the top bunk has gone to bed and the wire netting has sunk on to my head, so you'll forgive me, eh ?

Tell Billie Dad is thinking about her all the time, but cannot say much about her just now.

I am wonderfully well, absolutely great, and jake all round, and, with everybody, keen and hopeful of the future, and just tickled to death every day that I have left the base and am here doing a really bit.

As regards my wee personal interest in it all, it seems that my luck has been so wonderfully good all along that it must be going to stay with me. Let's hope so.

Good luck, Kiddie. Don't worry more than you can help.

Next Day.

It's about nine-thirty or ten—I've just got up (active service), made our bed, which consists of folding up four blankets and a rubber sheet, swept the floor (we soon pinched a broom). The floor is six by eight feet so sweeping is not exactly a killing job. The debris, as it does in all of France I have seen, is thrown in the middle of the street to wait for a horse and cart to take it away. Of course we only live amongst the working classes and the peasants, but I have never yet seen water laid on in a house. There is a well or a pump somewhere down the street, usually surrounded by very dirty and very numerous children, many as young as four years old, with all kinds and con ditions of pails and cans, usually far, far too big for them to carry. When you go to get a mess tin full, the majority of them clamour for "one cigarette" — "one pennee." The very youngest little girls smoke cigarettes without their mother's minding a bit. . . . I have yet to see a clean, fresh peach of a child. Of course you must have in mind this is war time, the people are dog poor, the men are away, the Germans are only three miles away. It is a mining district, and their houses are all occupied by "foreigners."

The fire is going fine. We got some lovely coal last night (after dark), and we just had two swell pieces of toast. W. swiped a can of real butter from somewhere last night. I see it was made in a hermitage in Brittany. On the toast, I had Golden Syrup, a ration now, and a good one, too. Also a quart of strong tea, and now I feel all jake and comfy. A fellow gave me a package of "Old Chum ", rotten stuff, better than the issue. I'm smoking your pipe — the old one. The only thing wanted to make the running perfect is the newspaper, but neither Sergeant T. or your noble uncle possesses three ha'pence to buy one.

In a minute I'm going to fetch a tin of water, put it on the stove and have a jolly good wash and shave. I even shine my shoes on this job. Before I go to work at one, I shall try a captured Spanish onion in a mess tin of bacon fat, a present from a friendly cook, also some slices of real ham (not a *present* from any one), have another quart of strong tea, and a piece of cake which a fellow got from home and gave me last night. Tonight at seven, I shall have a full course dinner at the Officers' mess at eleven o'clock. B. will have the bed down and a good fire left.

But remember; tomorrow, or the next day, or the next, my home may be a ditch, with a nasty German looking for my goat in another ditch only a few yards away. Sitting here in lazy comfort, it's almost impossible—that war is all round and up in the air. If I were to walk out of this door far as from 77 to Central Station, then back, and repeat the distance—I'd be in Fritzie's line.

Yet here I am in absolute comfort, with voices of women and kids on all sides.

No, I wasn't on the draft—I thought that I wouldn't be (I'm too valuable a man to send up).

Today there may be a letter. Always that's the main thought of the day. And when that day's gone, I always say,—"Well, there's tomorrow soon here."

Right after Easter Sunday, 1917.

My darling Lal: —

I was in the big scrap, right from the beginning.

Am writing this in an underground cave. I have no paper or anything. This should be the greatest letter I ever wrote you. . . .

I never got a scratch, though you can bet I had some near shaves. Holy Gee! and my first experience under shell fire, too ! I was plumb scared to death. I've got to admit it; but I think only I knew it. Long before you get this, of course you will hear the story of our advance. I told you it was coming quick; didn't I ?

Up to tonight, our division has two thousand prisoners, and they are still coming in. We have no news; we only know what is happening in our brigade.

The shelling is — well — I dunno' — there isn't a word. ...

I was ahead of the tanks.

They were no use — too slow.

The arrangements went off without a hitch; the barrage was exact and splendid. I never saw one Fritz plane all day.

I saw more of the battle than any other Canadian. I was detailed to carry films and plates for the moving picture man!

I volunteered for it — grabbed it awful quick, when I heard of it. I was ahead of the 29th, and we took a film of 'em, going in.

Remember, every Canadian and English picture you see of the battle, your Hub passed the plate, and stood there.

There's a lot of 'em, so look out. Try to see the Canadian Records pictures.

I am awful well — but worn out.

Our casualties have been light. The artillery did the trick. Every object was taken at the exact second as arranged — wonderful!

The Germans were a very fine lot indeed, clean and smart-looking; they were absolutely outclassed.

The photograph chap, a Captain, is absolutely fearless, and stood on "the top" to take pictures. I didn't let him beat me; I went where he went — but I dunno' how I got away with it.

Some of the pictures are to appear in the *Daily Mirror*.

I have lost all my kit — my razor — everything. Send me an Ever-ready Safety, please.

If only I could have got away with the souvenirs, I'm sure I'd be a rich man. The only thing I grabbed was a Fritz water bottle, as I was thirsty.

I had lunch in his third line trench on him: sour brown bread, two kinds of sausage — awful stuff! Cheese, two bottles of wine, and all kinds of cigars and cigarettes.

Our guns have advanced up in the open now.

I saw the cavalry go in.

You forget all about the machine guns and rifles; it's the shells. The noise is so great you don't hear Fritz's till it's on you. If you flop in time, you're alright; but the air is full of flying metal all the time.

We captured a big general.

One battalion captured a field hospital complete.

It was the biggest day of my life. I can't quite understand how it's possible to live through a day like that; but the casualties were really very light indeed. I am, for tonight, in a big underground cave with passages hundreds of yards long. I haven't shaved or washed for four days now. You are so doped with weariness and excitement that you don't worry about such discomforts. I have no idea what I am going to do, even tomorrow.

I don't know if the Canadians are going to be relieved, or not; or how far the advance has gone, or anything. You see, each brigade went over the top of the other; we hear the Imperials may go over the top of us.

Fritz still shells us all day. One dropped within thirty feet of me this afternoon, and I hadn't time to drop; but was never touched.

I think of you all the time, dearie, all the time.

I am as cheerful as I can be, and hoping for the best.

Don't worry, dear — please.

I am to be stretcher bearer with "B" Company of my battalion.

I met one of my pals being carried out by two Heinies — a lovely Blighty he had, through the flesh of the thigh. Lucky devil!

All the Fritz prisoners are nothing but stretcher bearers.

I can only wonder what Canada is thinking; but surely she is proud. It is a wonderful day.

Easter Monday—everybody so smiling and happy. Our battalion repelled a counter attack, and ripped 'em up.

I was right amongst a bunch of tanks, when Fritz got a range on 'em and fairly surrounded 'em with big shells. Gee ! I was glad to beat it.

It's very cold and snowy—confound it. *Au 'voir*, dear.

God bless you.

I think—Thursday after Easter Sunday, '17.
My very dearest Kid : —

I guess we'll go in again. In the meantime I am kept here with a party getting ammunition up from the cars—the most desperately hard work I've ever thought of—and dumping it outside. Climbing up is the hard part, and going overland seventy or eighty yards to the guns a little risky. Every day somebody gets killed. Yesterday Fritz wounded three of his own men who were carrying out our wounded, and killed one of our fellows this afternoon.

I was hoping we would be relieved, too, as I haven't washed or shaved since we came in. Water for tea has to be fetched in gasoline cans, two each, from down a trench a long way, just this side of Nouvelle St. Vaast—or what is left of it. I am quite well—very.

If the battalion goes in again in a day or so, I guess I'll go with them. They'll need us. I can't say I'm looking forward to it; but of course I understand what it means, and that it is what I am here for.

I wish it wasn't so cold. If only the people at home understand this war and what we boys suffer—and never a holler! How little I understood, even up to a week ago; yet I'm glad I'm here. It is my place.

The Fritzies here work very hard and uncomplainingly and willingly with our wounded; every one has remarked on it.

They were a fine appearing body, too, those opposed to us. Of course nothing could last under our bombardment. It was magnificent—awful. It was a walkover for our boys. Casualties were light, very; but of course—in proportion, I mean—

If only we could get news ! We know nothing, only rumours.

Yesterday I was over the No Man's Land (of yesterday). I found some cans of Fritz's bully beef—I don't like it much. But the desolation—my God, it's unbelievable! Even old skulls unearthed by shells—French—from the early days of the war ! And debris of every conceivable description, German and English mixed!

Our barrage was marvellous, a perfect curtain. Nothing could live, and nothing did. The prisoners surrendered from deep dugouts, or were smoked out, or bombed in.

Do you remember once telling me you didn't believe those moving pictures were genuine, that no one would risk his life for dollars ? I thought of that remark more than once on Monday — with a grin — as I followed Captain C. up "on top" to get a picture, when down in a shell hole seemed the only possible place. He was the limit, that man, brave as a lion. We got some splendid pictures, and of course you'll see them — both the movies and the official Canadian Records pictures. As I told you, I'm in several.

We had some narrow escapes, of course. Luckily we got inside of Heinie's barrage and were comparatively safe from shells of that kind. (It's queer how you forget machine and rifle bullets.) I suppose this cave will be used for other purposes now. One day I'd like you to come to see it. I don't think any of the battle fields can ever be used for agricultural purposes or anything again. You can't understand. No one can but those here. Every square yard contains unexploded bombs and shells and munitions ; rusty tangled wire is all over, and holes, — just all holes — that's all there is. Front line trenches are no trenches at all, really — only connected shell holes, half full of water.

How we exist, let alone "carry on", I don't know. Yet you never hear a kick.

For my own part, I haven't been tried out yet. I haven't done a "trip in", let alone "go over the bags." I can never be too thankful, though, that I saw this big battle as an eyewitness, right close up, and that you will have a picture record of it. . . .

Don't know the day but sometime in April — (ground covered with snow). We are in "Battle order" — no packs or blanket or anything.

My dearest Lallie: —

I have just spent the most gloriously comfy night possible tucked in a Heinie Officer's dugout (and they are some palaces) and have just heard the joyful news we are going "out." Consequently I am just delirious with high spirits. . . .

Lai dear, how I wish over and over and over again that I could tell you of all this. You know how interested I am in " things ", how I observe everything and immediately want to tell you of it. Yet — here I am, with so much to say, and can't, because there is so much.

I have read, with you, all the big descriptive writers' accounts of the "front line", yet no one has ever even begun to show me it, no one can describe it. You must see it, live it, and live it as a private in the line. Some one has said — "nothing is unendurable because all has been endured." That is true. I have worked till I thought surely it was impossible to continue, yet continued. I have lived through cold nights and wet and mud, and felt certain tomorrow would see me all in; yet I wasn't. Only one thing is as I thought; I fear the wet and cold worse than the shells.

What shall I tell you ? You don't want to hear about narrow escapes, and shell fire, and all that stuff. It's too common —

I'll tell you of little things.

The first night "in" here, after the big battle, we took up positions way over Fritzie's tenth or twelfth line. He was right to think Vimy Ridge untakable. It was. But a man can advance behind a shell curtain which does not leave a blade of grass (if there was such a thing) untouched. The enemy is *bound* to go to his dugouts, and as the curtain passes over him, all he has to do is to come out and surrender — those who are not buried. No one can blame Fritz for thinking we couldn't take this place. Machinery did it, guns and mathematical planning, in this instance without a mistake.

But — s'nuff.

Since the day I left our little comfy base, I haven't had a day from the Zone unless a dugout is "out of it." Fritz isn't bothering us such an awful lot; but he's trying to get the advanced batteries and searching his old lines and roads all the time. Of course he knows the exact positions, and it's trying.

The first night "in", I honestly nearly died with cold. Next day I was wandering around and found a practically untouched officers' dugout.

It's the limit, all boarded up, with a sitting-room, and swell bunks with shavings for a mattress. I told others, and a pal of mine, young V. R.; and we moved in. It's heavenly. The door faces the wrong way; but only a direct hit in the entrance could get us, and there are two entrances, so we could hardly get buried. R. and I with our two overcoats slept most absurdly comfortable; rations came up, even bread, and a letter from you, so we haven't a complaint—particularly now as we hear we are going out tonight for a few days' rest.

Water is the only difficulty, as we have to get it out of shell holes.

Yesterday I came upon some typewritten orders of Heinies, and handed them in——but I don't expect a V.C.

From this Ridge or series of Ridges, we have a wonderful view : a plain for miles dotted with untouched villages in the distance. On my right and left are the batteries—one an eight-inch of Fritz's own guns captured complete with ammunition dumps. These have been turned round and are pasting him night and day. It seems amazing that one can sit in safety fifty yards away, hear his shells coming and watch them burst round these batteries, knowing there is no need to worry—it's not you he's firing at. . . .

Did I tell you I actually found a Y.M.C.A. in a dugout in the very run of the advance. It's the limit. Of course it was in a safe place, but just the same, it was well up. . . .

Do you know I wasn't half so scared, that day (taking the pictures), as I was the day they put me on building the road over which they got guns into and down the Ridge. That was the devil of a job. The road runs down the side of the Ridge into the town and the valley below. Fritz hadn't had time to destroy it; but our own shells broke it up a lot while the boys advanced. Some three or four thousand men were put on the job of fixing it up — in direct view of Fritz. As they explained; the "guns must be gotten there." The holes were filled with anything at all. Old Fritz had had an engineers' yard down below, and threw all his material into the shell holes any how. Even as we worked, the guns staggered through somehow; the road was littered with dead men — dead Heinies left behind — and men killed as we worked. No one moved them; there was no time. In the side or bank of the Ridge were his old dugouts. Every now and then we dived for these; but you couldn't remain only a moment — the "guns had to be gotten through." I was carrying a long pole with another fellow; right in front were four men with a big beam. A shell killed three of the men in front, and blew us two flat, pole and all. I sure thought we'd got it. We dived for a dugout, falling over a dead Heinie in the doorway — it was his late dressing station —

now ours—and there was an M.O. calmly working on wounded as if he was in his surgery at home. Isn't it hell that the fellows who really do the work won't ever get the credit. One doctor sits safely at the base, another works right up; and no one at home knows the difference. However, we went back at last, and believe me I was tickled. I spent that night in a shell hole, and next day we went to the rear again.

No one knows where we are going, or anything.

April, Morning of the 22nd, "Out."

My dearest Kiddie:—

As soon as ever you see this paper you'll say all is K.O. and not only we are out safely, but I have got your parcels as well. Certainly nothing could possibly have been more cheery and ripping altogether than to have got them when I did. It was a direct hand-clasp from you, and I needed it, as you will guess. I was about all in physically, and getting to be something of a nervous wreck, too. But Oh! dearie, you cannot realize the wonderful change in everything now. Everyone positively radiates good fellowship. Already I have friends and am with a good clique. But even so, happiness—lazy, good-natured, carefree happiness—seems to have electrified the air. The sun shines. We have mail from home, hot tea, two blankets, newspaper—and up to last night we had nothing. I don't want to sound melodramatic, but you know death is in the air and all round, and though no one mentions it, even when some one suddenly goes West, it's with us alright. I know it is with me. Fritz gave us hell yesterday afternoon, and fairly sprayed our parapet and parados with shells. Our company, we now know, suffered most. At dusk, all were actively preparing for the relief, and wondering just whether Fritz would happen to choose the identical moment for a strafe. The relief was a trifle late, and the waiting, to us, trying. It was my first experience. Eventually the relieving platoon from the particular Battn. arrived, and came in the trench, and away we went across the dark plain in single file. — I say dark. It was never dark. Fritzie's flares are up, all the time. We got well away the first two miles, and then seemed to fairly walk into bursting shells. We made a tremendous pace, but somehow could not seem to get away from the screaming rush and *Rrrr – up* as they burst around. However, eventually we did get away, and at dawn pulled into our rest camp, a new city of tents, 'way in advance of our last resting place. The cook wagons had hot tea and bacon and bread and "mush" and jam, and we just flopped, and ate, and felt good-natured. Our bunch are not in tents, but under spread tarpaulins. It's alright — everything's alright. Later, we got two blankets and Cpl. R. K. and I doubled up and slept. Later, I borrowed a Gillette and shaved and washed in a shell hole half full of water; then we bought canned fruit and biscuits, and just lay around. Then we got mail—as I told you—and the world is good. Somewhere even, the Battn. band is playing, aeroplanes are aloft, our biggest heavies bark away; but Fritz doesn't send any over.

There is a fly in the amber—a big 'un. We go back in the line as supports to the attacks—they say tomorrow night; and we had counted on six days. Let's hope supports are well back and won't be needed. It seems to me there must be a divisional rest soon. The men are not at their best—it's a fact.

But of course the aspect of the war has changed now. It's of no use getting Heinie on the run, if we don't keep him there; is it? There are even rumors Fritz is beating it further back.

Don't worry about me. Think, as I try so hard to do, "it is written." Not many get killed outright, and by far the most get nice soft Blightys. Maybe I may be one of these. . . .

Remember this is the only place for a Britisher who is fit and well. That thought should be with you always.

You are always with me here, wishing me luck, and helping me to fight it out—

God bless you, Lai!

3 P.M., 26 April, '17.

My dearest Lallie: —

Our rest has now come to an end and I'm writing this while we are packing up. At six p.m. we beat it for the "transhays" once again.

There is a nice little rumour going around that we are only going into supports and this is borne out by the order to take our packs with us, not battle order as previously, so I have sneaked a blanket, and folded it inside my stretcher. I hope that's as far as we are going. Well, I hope I can jump that same Fritz dugout we were in before. I'll make an awful bee-line for it, you can bet on that.

It's very cold today, again. I wish the dickens we could have stayed a while longer under our "Bivy." Unfortunately, they didn't pay us this time out, so we can't tote any "eats" in with us. I have still some candles left, though, so we can warm up "mulligan", which is something.

Personally I have an awful hunch we shall ditch our packs in a couple of days and go through the old performance again of the last trip — reserves — supports — and front lines. . . .

Next Day.

My dear, I wish I could transport you over here for just one hour ('tween shellings), — so you could see how things are, — and then again I wouldn't. The sights are interesting beyond anything in the world, I suppose—yet—they are awful, too. Last evening in very lovely weather, we pulled out, leaving our comfy camp behind. Our new place—supports, or reserves, I don't know which—is on the old dead line of only the other day. This life don't seem to allow one to soliloquize or see things in retrospect; but, every now and then there's something hits you, and you forget your immediate troubles and see it from the outsider's point of view. Today as I looked around, it suddenly occurred to me I stood on historical ground. For two and a third years, the lines have never moved. France lost thirty thousand men on this very spot. England tried to take it and failed. And now Canada walks over it and digs about in it, uses old French rifles, torn up out of the ground by shell fire, for its dugout supports, and machine-gun shields as roofs. One day you must walk over the trail from Neuvelle St. Vaast to Vimy and remember— indeed it would be impossible to forget—that here Canada made herself ace high with France.

The scene is the most depressingly desolate it would be possible to imagine. The ground has only a few inches of loam over the chalk. It is honeycombed with trenches and tunnels, and— this is not an exaggeration—on the front four miles deep, (I dunno' how long) you couldn't find one shell hole six feet from another. The consequence is that, in colour, it's a sort of dirty pale grey; not a blade of grass or growing thing anywhere. The ground is littered with rotting French packs and equipment and German ditto and the more recent stuff of ours. It is a graveyard. Big shells have uprooted parts of bodies everywhere, and human bones lie dirty white in the open. Old-fashioned munitions unexploded lie side by side with the new, half-buried in the drying mud; the trenches are all broken in, gun emplacements—observing posts—sticking up in fantastic shapes, twisted iron—rusty barbed wire, rotting wire and splintered wood, add to the desolation. Tin cans with labels printed in French and English and German are everywhere; here and there a huge mound of white chalk in irregular shapes. These figured in the official communiques of over two years as "we exploded a mine in the Neuvelle-St. Vaast sector and occupied the crater." German and English both said this; in both cases it was true, as each lip was held by one side, it being necessary for the holders to cover their helmets with wet cloth and quietly peep over the top to snipe each other at forty— thirty—fifty yards range. My friend took me over the ground today, and showed me the different trenches they held last winter. Fritz was averagely thirty yards away; it seemed unbelievable that it could all have been so. It is beyond words to describe. Today we walk on the top, and light fires, and live in safety; yesterday, to look over the parapet was instant death. Here, too, I came out of a cave in the very bowels of the earth, where the guns only sounded like very distant thunder and walked about in a hell of sound, watched and helped take pictures of the boys going over and taking these very trenches, and saw the big battle won on the memorable April 9th, 1917.

France had big feelings about Vimy. Today Canada is getting the glad hand from her. I have heard of people, French people, stopping to shake hands with boys wearing the maple leaf down at the base—an unusual thing, as the French are most taciturn, not excitable as we have been led to believe. Not now, anyhow.

One soon learns to be resourceful and quick up here. Last night we arrived, piled arms, and "dig yourselves in where you can, boys" in an hour. K. and I had selected a corner in a broken trench sheltered from the wind, tore sandbags from dismantled parapets, walled it in, put the stretcher and the rubber sheet over the top of the roof, laid another sheet on the ground inside, got a blanket and our coats spread out, our kits for a pillow, a candle (one of yours) lighted and stuck on a stick, pushed between two sandbags at the head end. Our entrenching tools trans-formed a gasoline can into a brazier—wood is everywhere—quickly a good fire was blazing at the open front end, a mess tin of water boiled quickly and four cubes of your Oxo made us a good-night hot drink. We slept perfectly. Fritz threw over a few shells—apparently out of spite—but they were "tired" ones when they arrived, and didn't disturb us, nor the rats which were numerous. Early this morning, off came the temporary roof, a few hundred yards wide of scouting around, and we had a sheet of shell-torn corrugated iron, some broken trench mats, some netting wire for a permanent roof, the wall reinforced with more sandbags, another rubber sheet—no doubt belonging once to some casualty—for a door, and now we have a home to be proud of, where I am sitting writing to you. We put a row of sandbags on the top to make it solid and plugged the holes with mud. It isn't bomb proof; but only a direct hit can get us, and shelling is only most desultory, so we are safe as at home. Some of the boys have built most palatial places with lumps of chalk, regular huts. Fires are going everywhere; no one seems to give a damn about Fritz observing anything. In fact, all through I notice a growing contempt of him; it is taken for granted he is beaten and knows it.

The opinion is growing everywhere that Fritz cannot hold out. I wish I dare believe it. The guns are at him all the time; sometimes for an hour or more they all open up together. It is like a million big drums in the distance, punctuated by the leisurely whistling—sort of sobbing—

passage overhead of the very big fellows behind. The field guns are all away up; nothing can live where our artillery is — nor our organization. Only a few days ago, this was No-Man's-Land; across here now are a dozen roads, long never-ending lines of transports and pack mules — one road for "in", another for "out." Railway tracks have already been laid right up to the Ridge and over. One appears to have a number of gasoline tractors on it, small powerful engines ; another has big dinkies puffing away day and night. These lines of supplies are endless. Last night I noticed a pack mule train where you couldn't see the end nor the beginning, and it's level ground for miles.

I have understood that in the trenches on our right, the Germans made nine counter attacks in the last two days, and not one reached our line. The artillery cut 'em up, and the ground in front is a mass of dead.

I just decided to have a wash, so found a shell hole with some water in it and an old steel helmet, stuck it on our stove and had a beauty, with Pears soap and a clean white towel.

When I had finished, I got a hurry call: "Stretcher-bearer!" A sergeant of our company had driven a pick into a buried smoke bomb, and it burst in his face. It was very bad — very bad indeed. I could only bind it with a shell dressing to keep the air out till he reaches the dressing station. It's a Blighty one alright.

For twenty years to come, there'll be accidents of that kind happen all over the front line in France.

There were one or two "sticky-out" things I intended to tell you at various times. I'll try to think of them now. One was: Heinie has a new shell. When it bursts, out pops a terrifically brilliant arc light which hangs in the air far too long. The country is made as bright as day. Imagine the feelings of a bunch of men working, or marching in the open at night, and one of those damn things busting near! They flop, I guess, tout suite. We had one bust over us, but we were in the trench and so safe. It's a good one—and I fear, if only his observation is good, it will be a bother to us. Like every one else, you have heard of Fritz's gas shells. I was under the impression they were a fearsome thing. The other night, coming out, I noticed shells coming over and hitting the ground with a dull "flop." Soon I noticed a queer smell like—as much as anything—fresh green tree bark—laburnum trees. I said "What the devil's the smell.?" "Gas shells," some one says. Try to imagine us groping along in the dark in single file, tearing along all we knew, to get away from the zone of shells. Right and left, every minute, a big "Ker-up", as one bust,—each man looking only at the feet of the man in front, as the murmur continually passes down the line from man to man: "Shell hole on the left!" — " Wire under-foot", — " More wire" and so on, the only guide you have, and me bringing up the rear carrying a stretcher which sometimes got so heavy I thought really I could never make it. And then the guy says, "Gas Shells!"

Without stopping (I can laugh now), I lugged out the mask of my "gasperator" ready to put it on. However, I noticed the chap in front didn't seem to be worrying, so I let it hang. All the time, there was the whistle of the arriving shell, and the full flop of the shells in the mud and the smell growing stronger.

Well, — that's all.

They're a joke. Unless one comes and lands in the top pocket of your tunic, they're as effective as lavender water or eau de cologne.

They land in the mud and give a little kick — an explosion which draws out a cork or something — and out oozes Fritz's frightfulness. I am waiting to hear of some one getting gassed by one. K. just came in the dugout and I thought I'd ask him if he'd heard of any one. He says, "Yes, at the Somme, when he threw some thousands altogether." So that's it. I guess he hasn't got the guns here, so his attempts are a joke.

The rations here are already getting in their fine work — no butter — no jam — only biscuits. Already I'm hungry as a bear. . . .

If you ever hit one of our camps and saw the fellows go for those canteens, you'd have a fit. Our canteen sold five thousand francs worth of stock in three days, and no one had been paid. It takes anywhere from half an hour up, to get into one, owing to the line-up. Money outside your pay seems essential; but nearly all the boys seem to have some. I had ten francs this time out, and young F. W., who had a hundred franc check, gave me eight francs. Down at the base where grub wasn't the main thing, fifteen francs every two weeks was bearable; but here — well. It's no fun. For instance, a can of lobsters costs four francs and a half; cake is sold in portions not less than two francs' worth; a candle is five cents (Canadian); milk one franc and a half; peaches two francs twenty centimes, and so on. You can see by this how far a poor little fifteen francs is going to go. Next time out, we'll get paid; and we are already talking of our spread. It's going to include a packet of Quaker Oats, this time, with canned milk. I taste it now! Heavenly! . . .

My last thoughts will be of you, as will be my waking ones.

It is you I am living for — you I am doing this work for. When — if — the supreme test comes, I shall jump in, doing it with you by my side every second — remember.

Next Day.

My Very Dearest: —

The weather is still most glorious — sun — spring — lovely. You remember how I told you what a jolly camp we had ? Well, Fritz was over on his plane and must have made a picture of it, as I am sitting on our dismantled "bivy", waiting to know where its new location has to be. Heinie got too enterprising and commenced dropping shells amongst the huts, so we must beat it to a new home — only a mile I guess, or so, but it's a beastly nuisance nevertheless. Yesterday, we had a parade at two p.m. The Colonel just looked us over a bit, said we had begun to get the mud off anyway, congratulated us very much on the recent splendid victory, etc., etc., and told us he hoped we should not have to go in again immediately. *Tres bien!*

This morning at ten we fell in for a bath parade, about a three-mile walk. It was lovely, the bath and the walk too — and we got a clean change, leaving our other stuff behind. Officers and men just dig in together; all the saucy stuff on their part is [1] "napoo" here. We had the pipe band to play us down, too. All the Battalions have their bands here. We have two pipe and brass. Life "out" is positively blissful!

We have moved all our things over here now,

---

[1] *Napoo = Il n'y a plus.*

about a mile away. We packed our tarpaulin and pegs and everything over on my stretcher, about an hour's work — six of us — and we now have a ripping bivy. An old salvaged rifle holds up one end, pegs at the sides, ends fastened up with old tacks. The nights are very cold, and believe me we appreciate our little home.

The boys all seem to think the war is coming to an early close. I wish I dare think so. A captured officer told us that they had tremendous reserves for counter attacks. The more the counter attacks, the better, because the artillery will attend to them. But the main thing I think is to bust Heinie's morale to such an extent that his men surrender easily. I see they credit us with thirteen thousand prisoners, and now we hear Lens has given the Imperials six thousand more. One can take these figures without fear of exaggeration. Surely no army can stand this kind of thing for long. Then the French are after him for fair, too. No! I hardly think it can go on much longer. The points we captured were absolute fortresses; yet we took them easily. How can they hope to resist more, without their extraordinary defensive apparatus, dugouts and so forth? No words in our vocabulary can describe the artillery bombardments we put up. It isn't like a bombardment as you would understand it; it's just a noise continuous. You've seen mud, when it's in a jelly, sort of boil and waggle if you poke it with a pole. Well, I've seen the earth sort of boil like that. Of course, nothing can live in it, not a mouse. Then we have what the boys call "flying pigs", a thing like a torpedo that is fired in the air. When it drops, its own weight makes it penetrate three feet in the ground — the depth of an average dugout. It then explodes and leaves a hole like a mine crater. The Germans protested to neutrals about this thing; but I guess were laughed at, as I've seen 'em going up the line in hundreds. The finest piece of engineering work I've seen was the road from here to the Ridge to get the supplies up. The land from here to there was one mass of connected shell holes, wire, mud, and busted trenches. The engineers have made a road of rough boards where they couldn't do it without, and the impossible has been accomplished. Heinie has a better plane than ours. To look at, it's almost exactly like our new one; but for speed, he has it. I've seen him bring ours down in a sheet of flame, like a hawk on a pigeon. Just the same, we beat him in numbers. Often you can see twenty of ours up at once. He is over us repeatedly; but only in ones or twos, and never for long.

4 May, '17.

This is being written in a funk hole up near the front line amongst all the villages whose names are now familiar to you, where Fritz seems to be making a stand, and a pretty good one, too. Yesterday afternoon, they called upon us for a party to take water bombs, and machinegun ammunition up to the Battalion that went over in the morning. Of course, I went too. We hadn't been long on the way, before we saw evidence of what the morning's scrap had been like.

They made their objective all right — partly. Bombed their way to it. Even the terrific bombardment hadn't broken the resistance, which was fierce. I cannot say any more. Looking from the point of view of Empire, advancing against the might of an Empire, the move was successful. To our little unit of an army from Canada — well, we paid the price, I suppose.

Saskatchewan and Alberta did it, and there are three new roads on the maps of France which the kids will learn in their history one day: Alberta Road, Winnipeg Road, Manitoba Road, — and another less important one, Vancouver Road.

Though we made our goal with the stuff without a casualty, I dunno' how it happened. Damn the newspaper jays who represent us as "cheerful and happy as schoolboys going to a game" and all that slush! We can do the work — will do it — against any odds; but we are not happy or cheerful. We are in deadly earnest. Besides, what kind of a human beast can be happy and gay, when seeing his fellow Canadians being torn to pieces, and wracked with nerves!

We got back again without a casualty — our bunch I mean. Other companies were not so lucky, I believe. On the final bit of open before reaching our trench, K., who was in charge of the party, and myself were bringing up the rear, when a big one burst between us, I was half buried, was sure I'd got it; but neither of us had a scratch. We were greeted on our return with the news I half anticipated. We were to go back at midnight, to reinforce the other Batt'ns., who were going over once more to consolidate. Well, we made it. Only, once again the Sgt. and I got blown fiat. He says I'm sure one lucky guy, and I guess I am. May it last! I have a funk hole which I can just squeeze into. This afternoon I enlarged it a little, as two fellows in the next platoon, who were sitting in theirs with their legs stuck out on the trench bottoms, had their four legs taken off above the knee. One man was blown right on top of the parapet. We got 'em out; but I think there is little hope. Fritz is certainly pounding us, and he has the range to a hair.

This is a great war, to read about; but when you hear of these glorious charges, and all the rest of the newspaper gush, remember it sounds alright. It no doubt is alright. We are winning, not a doubt of it; but from the individual point of view gained on the spot, it's exactly what Sherman said it was. And then some.

It's about seven now, and we shall go for the rations when it gets dark — ('Tis the Lord knows what difference it makes whether it's dark or light; Fritz has his ranges all set. It's pie for him, all on his old ground, and he throws more over at night than he does in the daytime.)

The next letter will be written in happy circumstances — and all will look rosy and happy.

Keep cheery and bright. All is well as can be. Kiss little Bill for me.

Lots of really ones for you, and all my love.

9 May, '17.

Dear Lal: —

Well — we're out. I don't know how much you know over there about the recent fighting. I mean of this last week. I have a hunch, too, that letters from here are going to be pretty closely censored for a week or two, so I'll be careful, as I want you to get this.

We arrived out yesterday at daybreak. This morning I had my first wash and shave, and though feeling horribly "dopey", I'm much better than I was. We've had a "strenuous" trip, very strenuous. Some of the old timers say it has had the worst of the Somme beat. All admit it was

as bad. Some one is looking after me alright.
Never a scratch. I cannot believe it, and there is
no doubt whatever that at least on one occasion
I was in the very hottest corner of all. It happened K. fell sick—fortunately I carry a ther-
mometer—his temperature was over 103, so I
could get him out. The ass didn't want to go.
I helped him pack up his things, and right in the
middle Fritz opened up. I suppose it couldn't
have been worse. Personally, I was convinced
this was finis. K., of course, couldn't get out,
but hunched back in his funk hole with the rest,
and waited. I stayed in when I could; but of
course I was out a little "on business" up the
trench. The air was quite black; your mouth
was full of smoke. When it quieted down, K. got
out. And took my letter. Next day was not
so bad; but at dusk of course it started again.
Our bunch were to go up on a party to dig a new
front-line trench—our two sergeants were getting
the turn together—when a big one fell almost on
top of them. I think I've mentioned Mike to
you. I doubt if we could have had a better sergeant. He was a real friend to me, a stranger in
the Company; helped me in every way. Every
one liked Mike. It happened about twelve feet
from me. He was walking along the trench, had
just passed my funk hole with the other sergeant,
when the shell came. I felt it must have got
them. I went out. Only S. was alive; he was

terribly hit. Another stretcher bearer and I did what we could. I didn't see anything of Mike. There wasn't enough of him, I heard afterwards, to see. We got S. on a stretcher, and I helped get him out; but he died before we got anywhere.

All the time, we kept hearing we were to be relieved; but always they told us "tomorrow." One night, I was in the front line to continue it another hundred yards; that was a cinch. All we had to contend with were snipers. We didn't have a casualty. Next day, Fritz slowly moved up and down over it in a plane. Whenever there was a bunch of men hunched rather close together, he dropped a flare. The same second over came a shell, and—no trench—no men. I was in the trench the next night, beyond it to our. other Company to get out wounded. All the way, we climbed over dead bodies.

The salient is like a horseshoe. The heavies come from in front, the light from near-by behind. The trenches are not trenches, only two feet or so wide and about four feet deep. Fritz has every inch marked. These poor men—Why should it be *them* that line the trenches? I leave you to imagine what it's like, getting a wounded man out. The stretcher is wider than the trench. One night, we got on top to carry; we stayed about a minute. The first flare to come over, and he got after us with both whizz bangs and heavies. Right there is where a miracle occurred. A shell dropped amongst us, and—even now I don't understand it—it never went off. Not one shell in a thousand does that now. Well, we got out. Our stretcher cases were alive, and our "walkers" too. Going down the main trench, he shelled us all the way. It was the night of the relief, and we passed them coming up. Imagine that, too, if you can. The men hurrying, cursing, with sobbing breath, coming up; and we trying to get down with our stretchers. Telephone wires across the trench everywhere. I dunno' how it's done; but it is. When we got to our own part of the trench, another party took the cases and went on out. Our relief came about the same time. Our troubles weren't over yet, though. Fritz, of course, was wise to the relief, and, going out, in addition to ordinary shelling, put up a gas barrage (shells) away back. This we had to pass through. He threw a fearful lot, and it was pretty bad. However, we got through that, too. And, like a lot of drunken men, arrived at the point—some miles away—where our cook wagons were. I forgot to say it rained. Here we flopped in the road, and ate steaks and drank tea—then slept. Then came the really interesting part. We'd been asleep awhile, then were waked up to "stand to." Fritz had come over on those trenches and taken 'em. Now can you beat that? Personally, I couldn't either think or move, I was so "all in,"

Those poor devils who relieved us (Easterners) to crawl into those new trenches over all those dead bodies, find their places, and in the rain and dark, with Fritz shelling it, and then for him to come over ! However, in an hour or so, we heard they'd gone over and retaken them. If Fritz couldn't hold that line, under conditions as they are, having the ranges and everything — couldn't hold it from Battalions feeling as these fellows must have felt!—then indeed he is no good, and the war is over, as regards which are the best men.

Our machine gunners were the last to leave. They stayed to hold the line while the new bunch got all fixed in their places, so they were there when he came over. Our platoon gunner, it is claimed, held up the whole entrance. He claims fifty Fritzies, and he's no hot-air artist. He stayed till his gun was knocked out. It's a medal, sure.

The boys are not happy or jolly this trip out. There are rumours we must go in again before a rest. God knows how we'll do it. Today is the ninth, just a month since the advance; and we've hardly been out of the line at all. There's a limit, and I think we've reached it. Five million men they say we have. Well, where in hell are they ? Is it up to Canada to win this bloody war ? Nearly a month since we were paid, even.

It's silly, I suppose, to say, "Don't worry." '
You must do as I do — hope for the best.

12 May, '17.

My dearest Lal: —

I hadn't intended writing again till we came out. Rumours seem to be rather persistent that a little more is expected of us, in fact that there is to be a show, more or less big, and we must — I mean our outfit must — pull off the stunt. Of course we hope otherwise. I can't even tell you any of the details of what I have heard; but something is going to happen, I guess, and so I thought I'd better write you. We move up to-night, without our kits or anything, into another of those delightful ditches misnamed trenches, where there's no cover and damn little protection; where the whole works "stands to" all night and endeavours to sleep all day. We shan't have a kick unless we have to perform the over-the-bags stunt. I've seen an aeroplane picture — these are shown us regularly — of what's in front of us, and there's a row of machine gun emplacements connected up like this ══◇══◇══ running right across the picture.

H'ver, long before you get this, the scrap will be old, old news; and anyway, maybe they won't need us — this time.

Last night quite suddenly we loosed up one of our wonderful bombardments. No words can ever describe it; the air all trembles, and there is no distinction whatever between the shocks, yet so many guns take part in these displays that I am told one individual gun never fires more than four rounds a minute, and more likely only three. Of course they are more than wheel to wheel; they are in bunches, behind and around each other. When this starts, Heinie always gets the wind up for fair, and his trenches all along send up every S.O.S. signal he has: green flares, red flares, strings of all colours and shapes, and what with all these and the light in the sky from the guns and the roar, it's a scene like nothing that has ever happened before.

I have been under shell fire in the open and in trenches when only a few batteries were working, and it's rotten, to put it mildly; so we can all understand just what is happening when our guns turn on him with a regular performance. Frankly, I don't know what he does; I don't see what he can do. In his newer trenches he certainly can't have deep dugouts, and without these he's helpless. Funk holes are no good. So it's certain he must suffer terribly. Some day I expect these bombardments to break his spirit and cause a rout. I told you, I think, how he massed seven lines of men to retake Vimy Ridge and we caught them down in the plains below. They never even got within five hundred yards of it.

Though there is little to pack up, it seems to keep every one busy the day before a trip in, getting everything shipshape. I'm going to take two water bottles; I have a hunch there'll be rows this time. I have some candles left. We've been able to have a fire here, but of course one will be napoo up there. And we swiped some dry tea this morning. I don't think we'll be in long, anyway, even if we go over —

In less than a week I'll be writing again.

Au revoir, Lai dear. Remember I shall be thinking of you — you both — all the time.

Late afternoon.

I've had a lovely shave and wash. The towel, soap, powder, also the Gillette blades were an inspiration. After that I strolled over to the next trench behind us where B. is and lay in the sun and talked. Such are active service conditions — when the weather's fine, and Fritz is strafing some one else.

Casualties occur even here. While lining up for breakfast, this morning, a fellow just in front of me picked up an old, undischarged flare light. It went off in his hand, taking nearly half of it off. There'll be bad accidents here for years; the ground is a mass of unexploded bombs.

Evening.

Did I mention in one of my letters about sending some of that cocoa, sugar, and milk stuff.? They put it up in small tins, quite small. Send two or three at a time, four or five of those plain bars of chocolate, one can of Oxo, same as before, a small towel just the same as the last, no socks—got plenty—a few candles, and cakes. And cakes. And then cakes. Early and often.

Do you know I've come to the conclusion that you're a very lucky girl. I don't know any one else that writes letters, except when they are out. K. is engaged to a sweet-looking girl—at least her photo is sweet—yet he doesn't write as much as I do.

15 May, '17.

My very dearest Lal:—

Have just come down the stairs of a Fritz dugout— "safety first"—as the afternoon strafe has begun. We moved "up" to a delightful place all surrounded with guns, our guns, which Heinie seems to know all about, down to an inch, and keeps us in a perpetual state of flopping and "scrunching" up in funk holes, dodging shell slivers. Yesterday he kept it up off and on all the time. I had a very nice sandbag funk hole. It wasn't far from what was once a road. All afternoon he shelled where he thought batteries were; and as the nearest was at least fifty yards off, we felt fairly safe. Towards evening, I noticed that they seemed to be dropping closer to our "home." Good big rocks began to drop in it, and the concussion of bursts began to be unpleasant. I said to the fellows I was in with, "Here's where I beat it." And I did. They followed, as did another fellow in the next funk hole who had heard us talking. We just got a few yards, when two dropped in our late doorway. Can you beat it.'^ Is luck like this going to last." Can my hunches always be relied on? The fellow who had heard me talking and came, too, got hit. I had to put five dressings on him, all slight wounds. The lucky devil! Today he's laid in a nice white bed with a Sister handing him cool drinks. Why couldn't it have been me? It's all very well to be whole and unwounded; but this life is not exactly a rest cure, and anybody can have it for me. . . .

We have the Canadian papers now, giving the account of the Vimy scrap — rather amusing some of it. One of the papers said the preliminary bombardment lasted ten days. As a matter of fact, it lasted less than an hour; but it was the concentrated kind and evidently lasted long enough. . . .

One thing you said in your letter — that you supposed I would get hard and all that, through this thing. Well, the exact opposite is the case. The sight of this continual killing and wounding is making me madder and madder at such waste. I have even got where I wouldn't kill a mouse or a bird, if you paid me. It seems ridiculous maybe, but that's how it is with me at present. !;; Tonight I go on a working party, and I guess in a day or so we take the advance line, and in due course out again — the sooner the better.

19 May, '17.

This little bit of blossom was growing in a destroyed orchard, the only apple tree I saw alive in the village of Vimy. All the trees—those alive—are green now, but there are not many flowers. I saw a lilac bush one day. Such sights give you quite a shock amongst all the wreckage. By the way I forgot—I haven't heard yet if Heinie claims he has retired from here "according to plan" ; but if he says so, why did he— considering the shortage of grain in Germany and for obvious other reasons—why did he sow a lot of fields, even up to and on the Ridge, with grain ? It's just coming up nicely between the shell holes.

We have moved to a different line of trenches, much better ones this time, where you can light a fire and walk around. . . .

The weather has changed for the worse—not very cold, but raining and cloudy all the time. Your comfort seems to depend absolutely on the weather. Only very few of the boys pack an overcoat, and of course no blanket or anything. The other night, we were on a wiring party, laying barbed wire out in front. It rained all the time; in an hour the water was through every one's clothes. It would be alright, of course, if you had a place to sleep dry afterwards, but you haven't; you just dry out as you can. When we quit before dawn, we came into our funk holes and

just lay as we were. How you do it, I dunno', —
but you do and somehow no one ever seems to
even get a cold, but it's not pleasant. In the
sunshine, everything is lovely.

    . . . It is an effort to write and it should be a
pleasure. One thing, the interest, as a spectacle,
very soon goes out of the thing. From a
lookeron — a man on the staff — a newspaper
correspondent's view, it's all different of course.
We who live it and cannot get away from it, see it
with different eyes. Once I was wildly interested in villages and woods and positions; but I
find all that leaving me. A trench position has
an interest only in so far as whether it is usually
quiet or otherwise. As we hardly ever see a
paper, we know little as to the progress of the
war, so we never discuss it. Of course, the
everyday events of the life abound with incidents
of interest, many dramatic and humorous; but
when you come to want to write of them, a sort
of lassitude comes over you and, fight against it
as you will, it's no use.

    When you get orders for so many days in the
lines, you don't go all keen and excited, you
know, as if you were going to a party; though I'll
admit once I used to feel keen, keen to see it. Not
now, though.

    Tonight we go in for six days — I mean we go
to new positions for six days; we've never been
"out" yet; it seems a long time. But I hope

by then anyway we'll have the rest we've looked forward to so long. . . .

Kiss little Bill for me—tell her that Dad looks forward to the good times to come. Only last night I was planning a swell funk hole we'll make in the woods, one summer; and have a real camp out.

20 May, '17.

Last night, we got in without incident of any kind. It was a fine night, and we were in time to get a sleep. I am more than usually lucky in the funk hole allotted—at least by appearance. It's one of those trenches not connected by a communication trench; you must go overland. Mine is quite secure from shrapnel of the overhead variety, and safe even from shell fire of the other kind, provided they don't drop too near and cave it in. The trenches all along this new country are getting better and better. Each relief fixes them up a little bit better, until eventually they get to be regular homes and safe from 'most everything but direct hits. . . .

Rations are now getting like they are having at the Somme—abundant. I imagine the same amounts go to a brigade or division all the time. When a push comes and the numbers decrease, there's more to eat for every one. There was a more pleasant surprise, this morning, when gasoline cans of strong hot tea arrived—right overland—also butter and bread and so forth. It's amazing what a difference lots to eat makes on your outlook in the line. There was mail, too. I got a letter from B. with some more envelopes. He says his commission is gone through, and asked me to even picture him bathing in the sea in Blighty. Some fellows have all the luck. I miss K. this trip—another lucky devil, enjoying a course of some sort in a town away back, though another fellow we know well got shot to pieces with nerves and is gone to Blighty for a complete rest.

The chap bunking with me is an unconscious humorist, he just said,—"Gee, listen to those birds singing. I wish I was on my old chicken ranch, listening to them. Six days of this yet, and the world was made in six days!"

Mentioning the birds, it's curious; but you see 'em all the time right out in No Man's Land—the only things besides the slackers at home that don't seem to realize there's a war on.

My "roomy" is a philosopher of sorts. Lying on his back, smoking, he says, "Can you imagine anything more absurd than this : a peaceful summer day, and millions of men lined up, just like this, in holes in the earth, afraid to walk out in the field .'^ They call it freeing the world. The absurdity of, it all, as if we were born for this!"— and so on.

And—isn't it just too utterly absurd? A few men you have never seen, at a gun eight or nine miles away, send over a shell trying to kill a few more that they don't know and haven't seen either—and all the world busy at it! How preposterous, when we could all be enjoying life, and doing work, and good, around ! What thoughts crowd up when you let yourself think of it! The Fritzies in the trench over there don't really want to kill us; they want to sit quiet just like we do. They'd be just as sore as us, if anything started right now. Dozens of 'em are writing letters and reading just as we are.

Yet—we are the goats. The fellows who really want the thing are miles and miles away from the shells and the hardships. They know they will live, whereas I don't know I'll even live to finish this letter. After it's over, they win anyway—because we have lost years or months of happiness, and our health in any case impaired for good. The old times had it all on us. Their kings led 'em into battle, and took a chance, too.

Yet if I hadn't come, I'd have despised myself forever! . . .

Evening.

I notice I am getting most awfully thin. I guess that must be why so many of those nice bits of shell splinters don't plunk me. My luck simply won't go that way at all. A lovely opportunity occurred the other day; only about a hundred yards from the dressing station, I was talking to the two chief stretcher bearers—

everything all stage-managed to perfection. Heinie plugs a 4.1 over, and the two other fellows get the splinters. Now if I had just had a nice piece in the arm, had been all nicely fixed up and gone over to the dressing station, got the ambulance there for the clearing station, then the train—all French hospitals busy—so bang straight through to Blighty, then a nice stiffness would develop, a few boards, the first one, saying "I think this man had better go back to Canada." How's that for a nice little program, eh? . . .

22 May, '17.

My ownest Kiddie:—

Tonight we move on to the last stage and the most desperate one of our adventure.

It's raining, cloudy, wretched. Even in this trench where we have a roofed funk hole, it is bad. Up there, it will be unpleasant. It is our portion : days and nights spent in watching and waiting—the nervous strain about to the limit all the time. The regular trench stuff was a holiday to it. Then you went about your business peacefully, each side attending to his own affairs safely behind barbed wire. For diversion, both sides threw over a few trench mortar bombs, or made a raid, or something. The trenches were as near real protection as they could be made; moreover, the enemy not having been living there recently, didn't know more about your line than you did. There were communication trenches, and bays in the front line to prevent enfilading, and one shell was confined in its activities to the particular bay it dropped in.

Up here we have none of these things, no wire, no anything, just a narrow ditch. The material dug out, being mostly chalk, shows clearly like a dirty white snake across the countryside.

Nothing runs to schedule. Each side periodically gets "the wind up", owing to their state of nerves. Up go the S.O.S.'s and over comes the rain of steel and iron. If it's a false alarm, this gradually dies down like a storm, the flares resume their normal colour and regular frequency, and each side carries on — watching — waiting as before. Sometimes it is not a false alarm, and then there is "dirty work at the cross roads", and three lines in the newspaper the following day. ...

I shall always contend that the Canadians should not be sent in the same place twice. Their temperament is different to the English; they like change. Sitting under shell fire is not good for any one; but I think less good for them. In a war of movement and attack, they are splendid. Look at Vimy Ridge. Then again I may be wrong, because look at Ypres which has been all "hold." Still, a new front, if only a mile away, has an interest the old front has not. It is better not to know the danger, in my opinion. This is the last trip for a while, and a few weeks' polishing buttons and ceremonial parades will work wonders to our nerves. I guess it's all pie for us compared to Fritz. I don't know how he stands it at all. The more I hear of his last attack on us, the less I understand it. He came over in droves to occupy our trench — overland. He had no communication trench; there was nothing to gain; it wasn't a strong point. They must have known, even if they consolidated it, we should merely blow them out again with artillery. If the relief had not just been taking place, he'd never have reached it; as it was, he only held it an hour or two. Going and coming he must have lost a great many men — for what ? Of course, it may all have been part of a big plan of which I know nothing; but, on the face of it, it looks just like a useless killing for nothing. I am convinced now that he comes over, doped. Every one seems to agree on that. I guess he needs it.

Well, I didn't intend to write about the war — just a note merely — to say *au revoir*.

I know you would wish me a good trip — and a safe return. If you get another letter it will be from more cheerful surroundings.

. . . .Good-by, dearie — I'll be holding your hand.

28 May, '17.

My dearest Lal: —

. . . . The last letter I wrote was on the eve of going in; not in from away back, but in from another line of trenches. It was the advance point of the extremest advance point of the whole works, as it figures on the map of things at this time on our front — which I guess is the most advanced point that the British hold on the North Sea — And — well — here I am! That's the main thing. We are out and out for a rest. This is only our temporary camp. We are through — oh — ye — Gods! Through! Think of it! For — maybe — even four weeks. I could cheer on paper if it were possible. We are going back — back away from it all — back away from shells — and Heinie and all his works, and just get our nerves back. Since April 8th, I have not been really away from things; no one who does not understand can realize what it means. . . .

1 June, '17.

My very dearest Lal: —

I have only written one letter to you since we came out for our long rest. The joke is, there has been less spare time so far during our "rest" than there is in the front line. The first few days were taken up with our long "polish brass work", and rehearsing for the big brass hats' inspection. Finally the great moment arrived, and passed, just like any other inspection in Canada or England; though two months ago it was impossible to travel over the scene of it otherwise than down the connecting trenches, and, as it was, Heinie's planes were up most days. There was one big difference between the inspection and a similar one at home. There, every one would be grouching and kicking and cussing the whole apparently useless business. Here, no one ever let out a peep, not us. You bet we know when we are well off, and not a man wdio would not be tickled to death to go through all the harassing and irritations every day, for "the duration." No. Anything away from those shells, anything, has that beat.

I wish intensely — I could make you grasp the gigantic difference between "in" and "out", between a job behind the lines and one in them. There can be no state of life in the world where such differences exist, away from the war zone. This morning we started in our big hike to our resting village, bands playing, everybody happy, perfect weather. Today I have seen cows and chickens, women and children and little gardens for the first time since going up. This is a very lovely part of France (behind the lines). All the trees are in full leaf; May trees scent the air; old men are training the green peas up sticks in their little gardens, and tonight an old hen walked past me with a brood of chickens. All the men we meet—soldiers I mean—have the natural bearing and expression that we once had before we saw the line. You can never mistake a man who has been "in", no matter how smartly you dress him and polish him. Put him amongst a thousand who work behind, and you'll pick him out instantly. I have tried to define just where this difference is, many times, but I cannot. It's not in his face; our boys look the happiest in France. Is it in the bearing, the eyes—what ?

We are making the journey by easy stages. Our billet for the night is an old French farmhouse, built in a kind of square, the house, such as it is, with the doors built in halves like I remember our cowshed was at home. The other three sides by stables and barns, the whole of the centre of square being a large and very odoriferous manure heap. This reaches right up to the front door of the house; they don't seem to mind. On a board outside is painted *90 hommes*—1 bed. This doesn't mean ninety men sleep in one bed; the bed is for one officer. Our places are in the various "offices" in the farm. The old man made a great to-do about opening the door of his wagon shed which he had locked. No one could speak French; half a dozen officers had a try at him without result. Only more gesticulations.

Luckily a French Canadian passed and was commandeered, explanations were forthcoming, the door was unlocked, and the wagons pushed on to the manure heap and the men crowded in. The weather being so lovely, most of the boys are finding places outside for themselves; though we are travelling without a blanket—we are hardened. I have found an old buggy hood and a fairly sweet smelling horse rug. This I have fixed under a hawthorne tree in full bloom, and am comfy and contented.

The little village has been taken complete possession of by the men. The village green by the old mill is covered with the boys talking and sleeping and contentedly doing nothing. Every tree shades a bunch, the cook houses—or "mulligan guns" as they are called—have fired their rounds of stew and tea. Those millionaires with money from home have bought eggs and fried them, and all is peaceful and happy. The guns are already too far off to hear, and any man referring to the war in any form would be thrown down the well. The French women remind us sometimes, when they say, "are we from Vimy." The answer, "*Oui, Madame*" always brings a rather awed and satisfied "A—h." We had forgotten we took the famous Ridge,—and therefore "some" boys!

There is a fly in the ointment: no mail, and no money. Canadian mail seems to have stopped altogether, and money : Oh, if only we had some now, when we really need it!

And now I will turn into my "Bivvy." Tomorrow we pass on through the long lines of poplars to the next village, out, still further out. Thank God!

Next Day.

Well, we have arrived at our village and got all fixed up. There are four of us in our billet, an outhouse at the back of a cottage, with the chickens and rabbits for neighbours. Everything is "merry and bright"; all we need now is pay, and some mail, and I guess we'll get both. I only hope you have sent a parcel or two along, and written pretty regularly.

I think all we have to do is physical training, and there'll be games and sports in plenty; that is, unless there's to be another big stunt pulled off, when we shall be very fully occupied indeed going "over the tapes" — *i.e.* taking an objective arranged from aeroplane photographs. Before the last scrap, the ground was even exactly reproduced in a huge plaster of paris cast, every stone and rut reproduced to an inch, all from plane pictures. This thing is now an exact science.

I saw a great air fight, this last trip in, so close that the bullets from their machine guns plopped into the ground all around us, when their noses dived our way. The proper thing to do was to get into the funk hole — but I couldn't have done it on a bet. I was too interested, and stood glued up against the parapet. No one was brought down, which was a good thing for us, as they'd have come right on top of us. I guess there cannot be a more exciting thing to watch; the curves and loop the loops they made — there were eight of them, four German, four English — were positively the last thing in thrills. The whirr of the engines, the rattle of the machine guns, and the excitement in wondering when one is going to pot the other, and all, is just the limit. They were quite low, too low for us in fact. The fight took place over our lines, an unusual thing, and it wouldn't have happened, only our machines were not the latest type, and Fritz took a chance. After about three minutes of furious wheeling up, down and around, the four Germans headed for home. The air situation is entirely in our hands. We have a wonder of a machine, a thing that streaks across the sky just like a hawk. It's a peach, can make one hundred and eighty miles an hour, built in three decks. We are numerically superior, much so; we patrol the sky perpetually in formations, the fast-flying machines circling above them. In the earliest dawn or latest evening you see them, and at night you hear them; they are never out of the sky at any time. Fritz seizes his opportunity quick, and he has a very good machine, rushes in between patrols and rushes back. He has only to fly fifty-six hours to get an iron cross — (*official*). He patrols our front line a lot, which is nerve racking to the boys in, but always runs away as our machines approach. Making a quick, or even slow, trip over a strip of front line trench is easy, of course; the hard part of it is to leisurely circle around and round for hours at a time back of the enemy's lines. This he never does; he cannot. And we do, all the time. That's how far the superiority goes, which is being so much discussed — the reason of our heavy casualties is that we have ten machines up to his one and we are always out, where he only rushes in and out a few minutes at a time. Just the same, it must not be forgotten he has a very good machine and some good men, and often gets in some very good work. I am inclined to think he is handicapped for machines.

Our new O.C. was a private and wears the D.C.M. won while in that trying capacity. He's a splendid man, easily the best O.C. in the Battn. and an officer has to be some good fellow to get the confidence and liking of his men in the line.

Usually after about the second day we are out, they discover they are "officers" and act accordingly. In the front line, they share their cigarettes and water and your funk hole with you, and talk, and ask questions from the sergeant about what they are to do. About the most insignificant thing in a front line is a platoon officer, while he's there; when he's out, he's a tin god again.

When they went over the top in the big show, our officer — not the one we have now — started to give orders. The sergeant says, — "Hey." Puts up his hand. "*I'm* running this show." And he did.

I've seen a newspaper most every day for a while. I dunno' how things look to you; but I'm not awfully impressed. I think they're just filling us up with hot air about Russia. In my opinion she's a thing of the past, as regards a factor of this war. The States seem to be backing up fairly, and are going to be a most valuable ally — much more so than I first thought. I bet they are going to do something anyway worth while. One thing that seems plainly obvious to one is that there's another winter's war ahead of us, and all of next year most likely as well. The handwriting on the wall is plain enough to see.

I think of you hundreds of times a day, and long to be able to plan. But — !

Tell Billie I am thinking of her, and loving her, too. Kiss her for me.

And to my dearie — just all my heart.

9 June, '17.

My dearest Lal:

Well, the leave is a thing of the past. Nothing to look forward to but the end of the war, I guess.

When I got back, last night, the Battn. was in the same place; and I was more than glad, believe me, as to have gone direct into the line would have surely been the limit of contrasts. Even in the short time I've been away, I seem to have lost touch with it all. A dozen times I started a letter in London, but never finished it; it was all so different, all of it, that I could never concentrate. I stayed at the Club all the time, the one in Charles St., Lady Drummond's house, and had for a companion most of the time an officer in the Flying Corps. We met in the Club; he had once been a private in a Canadian Battn. and was waiting for a transfer to the American Flying Corps. He certainly was a nice boy, in a "nice" way, as also was my other companion, a sergeant I met in the winter. He was over in London for a commission — and we all went everywhere together. I guess we saw everything worth seeing. We saw a show of some sort every day. And I have never seen such turns — never. Of course I was prepared to like everything, but I'm sure I never saw better; the music, everything, the dresses, the lightness, and brightness of it all. I couldn't get it. After this. It came as a shock that our life together ought to include this. I was homesick as the very devil; often I wished I had never come — I wanted *you*.

Not once, but a thousand times, I tried to grasp the fact that so few miles away a hell was raging

—and couldn't. No wonder these people don't understand. How could they." Lovely silk clothes and flowers and fruit and happiness don't "jibe" with "the line."

And the life of the town, at least on the surface, is just the same. One seems to half expect them to go about in black, be mournful, and serious, and grim, yet I suppose theirs is the better way. It makes you feel mad though, too, sometimes, to see so much happiness and flippancy. It did me, anyway; yet I would hate you to be unhappy just because I am here. Never have I seen so much gayety and richness of apparel, and spending of money in London before. The shops are full of the most expensive things; flowers and expensive fruit, and "eats" of the most elaborate seemed to me more common by far than before. And the prices — Good Heavens — I wouldn't have believed it. I can't think where the money can all come from.

When I was over in Blighty, I went to see a boy's mother for him. She made me stay all night and was so hospitable it was painful. Remember, I had not spoken to an educated white woman since October last; and then suddenly to be transported into the midst of a "nice" family —the experience was overwhelming. Such things would be alright and natural, if you hadn't all the time hid in the back of your mind that in a few days you would be "out there" again. And all at once I used to think of you, and what we might do, if only I was back—and then again, I would wish I hadn't come. No! "Leave" is not all it is said to mean. The old lady was very worried. She was the first woman I have been in touch with, who was afraid for some one loved out here, and I can see it is no cinch sitting at home. I think it brought you and me a little closer. I could see your view. . . . If they would conscript wealth, property, as well as men, we wouldn't need the men. The war would stop, tout suit.

24 June, '17.

My ownest Lal,—

I seem just now to have so much to tell you that I don't know where to begin. As you know, we are on rest, and altogether having a ripping time—only a little drill or lectures on specialty stuff in the mornings, the rest of the day off. There is a lake close at hand, though not a lake similar to yours. I mean there are no trimmings, no boats or anything; it's just a small French village in the mining district, but all the surrounding country is glorious, nevertheless, and there are no stray shells—most important feature of all. All the boys are enjoying things finely. . . .

Everything just now is devoted to sports—

Inter-Battn., Inter-Brigade, Inter-Division. The finals were all in our grand sports day yesterday. Of course, every one is a most enthusiastic booster for his Battn., and it's all been most exciting.

It took place at this very village where I've been all winter. When I got there, the village was a mass of men all on holiday; every Battn. came to cheer its men in one event or another; but ours mainly to get that ball game. It was great, just like a big Sports at home, only there were no girls or women; the field was surrounded with trees, an ideal place. All the big brass hats and every one was there, and out for a good time, and I sure did enjoy it. The (page cut by censor) know how to stage-manage a thing of this sort, and they went the whole hog, even to having the theatrical bunch dress as girls and stroll around with sunshades. Well, we won the ball game. We didn't do much in the running races; our Battn. doesn't run, we stand fast!!! But we won the heavyweight boxing, and the tug of war.

All the time I was running into fellows I knew. It was a thoroughly jolly enjoyable day. I wished a hundred times you had been with me. I guess there will be a day or two like that, though when the big bunch go back to Canada; and then we'll see it all, together—because I'm coming home alright. I'm getting some of your optimism.

Later.

Poor old Lal! I haven't finished laughing yet at your idea of a good war story. . . . But for your information, as it directly concerns my own job, stretcher bearers don't carry morphine; they carry—I carry—bandages, dressings (shell and field), iodine which I slash liberally on every wound, a pair of scissors, and sometimes a little sal volatile. That's all. . . . Imagine, before going over the bags, sitting in a dugout writing a lot of trash, and licking up the envelope. Precious lot of dugouts a private is ever allowed in! Moreover, you don't take biscuit boxes in the line; they go up in sandbags. And taking a blanket over the top is too funny. If you want to read front-line stuff, read Ian Hay who has been there—or, for a change, the personal experiences of Mrs. R. A. L.'s husband. By the way, I see you like my descriptions. I'm glad; that's why I write 'em; and if you didn't, it wouldn't be any fun. (Will you keep them for Bill when she grows up?) I'm just beginning to get used to things here again; the awful contrasts of home life and this are beginning to fade from my mind. Luckily, I didn't have to make the jump from England right into the line, but shall reach there by easy stages, so to speak. It isn't really bad here at all; in fact, it's just heaven after the line. But compared with life amongst equals and with freedom — of course it's awful.

I know the present is rotten for you, dear, in every way; but we must "carry on." It's all we can do. So I'll be where I won't have time to think of anything but life and death, eating and drinking to live, and being dry and warm— just an animal — a hunted animal. We all have our worries. Remember only to be alive is something to thank God for.

The photographs of you are simply splendid. I fell in love with you all over again. You are the "Ideal", the only one, and will be till I die— and I hope afterwards. Remember hard — always — that, if I should happen to have to pay the sacrifice, my last thought will, my very last one will, be loving you and hoping that the rest of your life is to be happy. Don't take this in a morbid spirit. I don't mean it that way at all. Already I have experienced moments which I was sure were "the" one. It wasn't, as it happened, but I was thinking of you hard. And I repeat my love will go out to you then, as it does now when I am alive and gloriously well.

It is because I love you so, and want our home so much, that I want to get through with this thing so badly.

You are worried about the political point of things, the "human" view, the reasons. I am concerned alone as to whether we can manage to pull through, while doing the day's work. I have done my "day's work" here satisfactorily; I know that. I have heard from several sources that I have "made good." It is enough. All we want now is for it to end — and begin our lives again; isn't it?

25 June, '17.

. . . We are trying to take the Americans seriously. I see their war loan was oversubscribed. Moreover, many things we read show they mean business. I see we are not to have them on our front. We had heard that they would work with the Canucks; however, I guess the French need them most. If only they could get here this year! But I guess it's impossible. I hope they can get that big bunch of planes over that they talk of; they would be invaluable. Isn't it amazing Fritz doesn't see, and realize.'^ I can't make it out at all.

I bet the Yanks show the English and Canadians how to handle the social end of things for their men. They'll make mistakes, of course; but you can't beat 'em at anything I've seen yet, when they go in for it thoroughly, and now it's apparent they mean this, mean to go the whole hog, good luck to 'em! I suppose internal affairs must be the very devil for those in authority to handle. There again they'll win out. They have a rough and ready way of dealing with trouble which is barbaric, maybe, but effective; and you can't go to war with kid gloves on.

I was in Blighty when the big scrap came off that straightened the Salient; some show I guess it must have been, too. Of course, I knew beforehand all about it, so it wasn't a surprise. I'd like to see the crater. Poor old Heinie! And the worst is yet to come. His line must break soon, I firmly believe; though that there will be a rout or general clean-up I very much doubt. It's the time it takes to bring guns up that holds advance back. The difficulty is to keep the infantry from advancing too far.

29 June, '17.

My dearest Lal: —

Well, the inspection came off as appointed. We were lucky in having it come early. Every one had prayed earnestly for rain; but apparently in vain, as the weather was lovely. I can forgive our Colonel for getting so particular and anxious beforehand; he evidently knew his man. I suppose the proper word to describe it would be *thorough*. We had other names for it, though. He examined odd links on the chains of the transport harness; dived underneath one of the water carts to fetch out a rifle in a case, a rifle which is never used (he found it clean); swooped on an odd man here and there and gave his rifle the going over as if he was buying a priceless diamond, strolled innocently past a platoon and gave the order "Gas!" (which means they had to get their helmets out and on in a given number of seconds). Oh ! he was thorough, alright.

When it was our turn, he wanted to know how many casualties we'd had among our number in the big show on the 9th April; said the number was too many; wanted to know just what was in our medical bags, and many other things. Finally, to every one's utter relief, he beat it, to inflict himself on another Batt'n in the Bgd. We hear he was pleased. So were we—when he went. And, just to spite him, we haven't polished a button for a whole twenty-four hours. He knew his job, though; you must hand him that.

Ever since, it's rained like the devil. Last night, I was thinking how impossible it is for an outsider to realize the meaning of life as it really is in the line. Those new trenches must be full of water, the life must be horrible in the extreme; yet we, who are just now under a roof, hardly think of it. Only a few—a very few—days separate us from it; yet you never hear a word mentioned on the subject. If we who know don't bother to think, how can you expect people at home to realize, who have never seen or ever suffered like discomforts? It's a thought worth pondering over.

Sunday morning early, 1 July, '17.

My ownest Kiddie, —

Tomorrow we *parti* for the trenches once more, and today we shall be decidedly busy. It's Sunday, and we have an important Church Parade—a Brigade parade—and who do you think is to be there? The "Dook." Quite like old Canadian times again. I didn't know he was in France. Packing up will not take long; but, just the same, it is always a rush. There is none of that ceremonial regimental stuff about it; you pack it how you like, ease and convenience alone count. . . .

The weather is rather cold and wet, and we'll miss the roof overhead pretty badly, I guess. Fortunately I didn't ditch my sweater during the hot weather, as every one else did.

You will bear the date in mind, and remember the news of this time when you get this. Things are stirring in our section with a vengeance; the guns are going incessantly. . . . It is just possible we shall be left more or less alone in the front line, Heinie being more concerned about the guns hindering his retreat.

I wonder how they are going to explain the loss to the rank and file in Germany. Human nature is pretty much the same ail over, and it is — must be, in fact — that the soldier cannot feel cheerful about these continual retreats, even if he implicitly believes that they are "according to plan." I know how we should feel, and it would not be good, and it would not help us to "carry on." I have been in this sector since the beginning of April, and I know that we—the guns and ourselves—have made it absolutely impossible for human beings to stay where they were. The true facts of the evacuation—whatever will be said (I am writing before the fall)—are that the enemy has been and is outclassed in every branch of war. In plain words, he is retreating because he has to. It is slow work, must of necessity be; but humans cannot stand this kind of thing for ever, and I look for a break, a bad break, somewhere in the line before October. If the Germans haven't realized by then how foolishly they are trusting in a broken reed, then we must sit down and endure another winter. The thing that never fails to be amazing to me is that the German people cannot see things as they are. However, I'm not very interested in the larger aspect of the war. To me, it amounts to whether I have enough dry pairs of socks for the wet trenches I shall so soon be in; if he will shell us heavily; if we shall be within his trench mortar zone (very important this—his "sausage" is a fearful thing); how far the front line is from the jumping-off place where you store your packs; will it be possible to get bread and fresh meat in to us? How far will we have to go for water, how many days will constitute a trip "in", and — never expressed, but half thought of in the back of the brain — will this be my Waterloo trip? What the politicians are doing, and the General Staff planning don't interest us for a second.

Afternoon, 1 July, '17.

The parade this morning was quite a surprise to me. Apparently it's Dominion Day — no one knew — and when the Batt'ns of the Brigade had formed a square in a pretty field surrounded with trees, motor cars came up and discharged about all the brass hats in France, including the Commander of the First British Army himself (the Canadians are attached to the First Army). Note that ours of all the Canadians in France, was the Bgd. chosen for him to attend. We even had special "programmes" printed, one of which I enclose as another souvenir. Photographs and moving pictures were taken, and our fastest and latest type aeroplanes made rings round the affair in formation, in case Fritz should happen to take a look over. The band supplied the music. We like our own band; but it doesn't compare with theirs.

It was impressive and interesting. The "Big Gun" made a speech in which he said the Vimy Show and later the (censored) one had plainly shown us that Fritz was getting less inclined to put up a stiff fight when we meant real business—he didn't tell us when the war was to end.

During the "rest", the specialty training— bombers, machine gunners, rifles, grenade men, etc. have worked on a competition basis for prizes—and after the parade the Colonel presented the prizes. There were eight prizes for the Batt'n, and notice this—"B" Co. took five of them. . . .

All the games and sports stuff and putting everything on a competition line is good in every way, makes the fellows keen, sets up friendly rivalry, and is interesting for every one. The rest has undoubtedly been a great success. The only kick the fellows have is that there were only two pays of fifteen francs each. I think that rotten myself; they could easily have slipped in one more, or even two.

Later.

They have recently got more particular about wearing your identification discs in the proper place, namely round your neck. You have two out here, a red, and a green. One is buried with you, the other—I dunno' what becomes of it. I've always carried mine in my pocket— though I wear a little medal affair on a chain round my wrist. At present, I am using a piece of old string off a parcel for the two round my neck; but if you like to send me a nice piece of silk cord, strong enough not to break, and durable enough not to object to soap and water, yet pretty enough to remind me of things "nice", I'd be tickled to wear it.

They have this moment come for our one blanket—sure sign of a move. A cold night on hard bricks tonight; better than mud, though.

I have really got hold of a *Saturday Post* with a yarn by Gardner in it. Reading matter has been terribly scarce here all the time, and to have a Post is to be in real luck—though somehow looking at the ads and things always makes me homesick. . . . It's all so different, like going on leave; the fact that people have comforts and luxuries, can he free, hits you like the concussion of a shell. I don't suppose you'll understand this ; but at times, when things are quiet, like just before going to sleep or dozing the day through in a funk hole, my mind automatically flies to you, and times we have had together, and what might be—if. Always—no matter if it occurs a hundred times—I hastily push the thoughts away from me, feverishly think of something else; but it never really goes. It always stays sort of behind in my brain, and worries me and keeps me awake. The fact is, I think of you as little as I can. I dare not give myself the luxury of it; things that I see and do, I immediately arrange to tell you of in the only way I can—like this,

"Somewhere else", 3 July, '17.

How I am to get this mailed, I dunno'; but mailed it is going to be. Yesterday we moved as arranged, and after a somewhat hard march. It would have been easy, had we not run into a road closed for troops "owing to being under enemy observation" and had to go some miles round. There are crops back there, every last inch square growing something, and it is not permitted to go shell-torn in the usual way. In the centre is the remains of a huge chateau, one of the biggest I've seen. A whole Batt'n can —does—billet in the stables and grooms' quarters. . . .

Last night, I talked to a fellow who had been up there. This fellow said we were all in holes, not connected at all, in the suburbs of the "big burg"; that it was impossible to keep men there more than twenty-four hours, as they couldn't get supplies in to 'em. That all was going well, we were advancing; but it was hand to hand stuff, and bucking machine guns, and Heinie was standing good.

How the devil am I going to get my wounded out? . . .

Well, tonight we'll hear again the sound which no one has ever described correctly, but which reminds me of a train coming towards you, as much as anything; and then, as we advance closer up, a thousand woodpeckers will seem to be digging steel beaks into iron. Both are bad, but I think I prefer the machine guns; they give you such nice aseptic "Blightys."

I have no "hunches" again this trip. Young F. says he thinks a man who is going to be killed gets a hunch. I dunno'. We shall see.

I am better equipped, this trip, with bandages and supplies than I have ever been, and I am glad, as I think I shall need 'em. Also I am comforted to know I have young F, as my "understudy." The rest is, as you've said once, "on the knees of the gods." . . .

Well — dearest — *au revoir*. It isn't good bye, even for more than a day. I'll write something up there, they can't do much scrapping in the daytime, I expect.

Keep as cheery these next months as you know how — and you *do* know how if you try. . . .

Kiss Billie — for me — many times.

8 July, '17.

My Dearest Lal: —

I have just been lying here soliloquizing on the curious ways some things work out in life, and how the devil it can be possible that all is working out for the best in this big world-cleaning. In my platoon is a human soul sent up from the Two Hundred and Umpty something

Batt'n, who is just—nothing. No brains, no evil, no physique, no anything—just half born. Of course, nevertheless in a trench, worse—a danger to others. In a recent lecture in which the lecturer referred to the enemy always as the *Boshe,* he asked what a Boshe was! A job is open for a man to look after a graveyard behind the lines. He is given it, a heaven-sent chance to strike him off the strength of the Batt'n. Moreover, you can't quarrel with the action. It is obviously correct. Yet—and yet—think! To be a degenerate is lucky. He will see his home in Vancouver; *he* will go home to all that home means, and no doubt talk largely of his experience—he made one trip "in"; and the man who is scrupulous to do his bit conscientiously, is physically fit, in other words a good man and a good citizen, he is the one chosen for the hardest part, his the life needed to pay. It won't bear thinking about.

Think, all my life I have taken, always taken; never given. And now I must give, give all, all the time; and there is no quitting. It is a joke, drat it, and a good one.

. . . I have read all the best descriptive writers on the front-line stuff; but not one of 'em has ever given a description of trench life as it is. They confine themselves to the spectacular deeds: the attacks over the top; and weird stunts where men win medals. That isn't this war at all;

those things are all easy, as men do them when keyed up to the proper pitch. All those things are great events in the history of a Batt'n. For instance, my Batt'n only went over at the Somme, and has only pulled one stunt since: namely, at Vimy on April 9th. Yet when you hear the boys talking together of the bad times, those things are not mentioned; because they were not the bad times. They were easy.

The newspapers ring with the wonder of the Vimy achievement, yet I haven't heard one say a word about our trip in May, when we held the line just by sitting, day after day and night after night, getting killed without firing a shot — just holding on. It wasn't spectacular; yet that was typical of the whole war. That's what it is; the other things are episodes, rare ones, and the correspondents make the people imagine that is what makes their boys' lives at the front.

I remember on the day and the subsequent days that we were taking Vimy and the plain beyond, watching the ammunition and water going up to the boys as they advanced. Previously, vast stores of trench-mortar and machine-gun ammunition had been stored, together with water in gasoline cans, in a cave only a few yards from what was then Fritz's front line. Fritz was quite wise to this cave, and guessed the use to which it was being put, so a battery of heavies was put on to shell round the entrance, day and night. The supplies were brought up and dumped in a heap near the mouth, and men with mules loaded and took them away, marching along right into the barrage which kept going perpetually further up, with the idea of stopping just this very thing.

The weather was awful; the ground was covered with snow; all around the mouth of the cave lay dead men, and more along by the dump, there being no time to move them. The string of mules would come up, one man to one mule, load up hurriedly at the dump, and file away into the row of black spouting craters which was the 5.9 barrage put up by Fritz. In time, they would come back through the barrage again for another load. The officer would count them, and say nothing, and every now and then go into the cave and telephone for new mules and new men.

This went on night and day—more in the night—for three days without ceasing. I know, because I carried the stuff from the cave to the dump, and every trip across that open strip of ground was an adventure.

Yesterday, I was reading an account of Vimy in *Canada*. He described it more or less accurately, missing, of course, the *heart* of the thing, the *little* things, as they all do. One passage he wrote from the Ridge, looking at the plain below, and casually mentioned "I saw a pretty bit of shelling" (by Fritz) "on a railway culvert," Yes, very pretty. There is a railroad embankment there which once hid his big howitzers. Now, however, instead of strengthening it, he spends many shells trying to break it up. And there is a culvert which received some "pretty shelling" twice. On two separate trips in, I have occupied the funk hole nearest to that culvert, once on one side and once on the other. I have seen seven men knocked out with one shell there — truly "pretty shelling." I have spent in all eight days and eight nights by that culvert, and run under it countless times. Not until some one can write and tell people what it means ; to sit or crouch — or squirm — around in one place for days, under continuous fire, without being able to go away, will you people at home know the war as it is. But — maybe it's as well they don't know. . . . Sometimes the correspondents are really amusing, — as when they have us "laughing like schoolboys, before going on a raid", and things like that. I may be wrong; but I don't think any one has ever seen one of the paper men in the actual front line. And I have yet to see any man laugh, while there. The atmosphere is tense with something quite different; a raid or patrol is gone on with the seriousness which facing a quick death entitles it to. Men don't laugh in the *front* line, ever. They "grouch" — a lot — about the food, the shortage of water, the weather, the insects, and many things besides. They kick like hell when our guns open up from behind on Fritz's line. Yes, I mean that. I guess you'll wonder why that makes us sore but it does—damnably. Because—Fritz will retaliate. He may suspect a raid. If so, up goes his S.O.S. amongst all the other flares, and down comes a barrage of heavies. Ours increase, the air throbbing and alive with the screams and hisses of different calibre shells, punctuated with the harsh tapping of hundreds of machine guns sweeping the open. It dies down a little, then increases worse than ever, finally to die down for good, when all goes on just the same—only that tense, whispering sensation in the air which is there all night, every night. For an hour or so, out of the dark, parties of four go down the trench, muttering and swearing, carrying something— "Look out there—gangway for a stretcher." The dead stay where they are, with a rubber sheet or an old sandbag, to cover their faces. Later, maybe that night or the next, a fatigue party will climb over the parados and scratch a grave a few yards from the trench, cursing the flares, and flopping, as Fritz plays a machine gun casually, just on the off chance, all along the ground behind, as a man might play a hose on a lawn.

These graves are not marked. How could

they be? Some one takes all the letters and things out of the pockets; eventually, if the man who has them doesn't get blown to pieces, they reach the Quartermaster, who sends them home. Some one writes a letter, and that's all. No advance, no spectacular raid, not even repelling an attack. So many dead Heinies, so many dead Britishers. And so she goes. And such is "a trip in."

Next day, 9 July, '17.

I put in a most delicious night, we pulled down our tarpaulin cover and made a proper "bivvy" out of it; banked up the sides and covered the ends, fifteen of us. Most of us had parcels. No one had candles, though; but I came along with those. Some one had *café au lait*. We made a little cooker. (I'm an expert, now, turning a bully beef can, a bit of sandbag, and a candle into a cooking stove. I used them right in the front line.) Every one had a cake, and cigarettes, and all; we were a happy bunch. I guess the front-line boys will make the closest fraternity ever seen, after the war; you get to know a fellow through and through in half an hour. But it is just as I thought: only the men who go in and actually do the scrapping know anything of the war. Any one can work; but when you work, and while working every second stand a chance of a sudden death, it's that that seems to count, and I guess it's only right it should. Today we have parades, parades, trying to get the mud off: the first at ten, another at two. It takes two or three days to get the mud off.

It's glorious sunshiny weather. This afternoon, there may be a pay parade. Up the line there is no regular pay-day; you may get three a month, you may get only one. There is no town here; but Y.M. tents and our own canteen, where you can get canned goods. The boys generally spend the whole works at once, and have one good feed. I guess it's the only way. . . .

The standard of duty, conscientious duty in the line, at any rate in this Battn. is very high. I told you I was a stretcher bearer. The vacancy occurred in the big scrap Easter Monday. A fellow called C, an original man, through all the scraps had the place I now fill. It is not a sinecure, but its dangers and hardships are lifted in a different plane from mere work.

When my Company took its objective that day — the point was the brim of a ridge — they went a few yards too far. The Bosch was running, and they followed. C. had been very busy up till then; but his big effort was to come over the brow. The Germans had some batteries — what we call whizz-bang guns (about fifteen pounders). These were not all out of action;

but when the gunners saw our boys coming over the edge they saw all was up, and decided to die game; so, instead of shooting over away back, they turned the guns direct at a few yards' range pointblank on our boys. Many were hit. It was "Stretcher Bearer on the double!" from point to point. Poor C. did what he could; he dressed a few. It was finished, anyway; no one could live, and he was killed. He might have got a medal! He did good work in the Somme, too. One or two very brave acts don't win medals now; consistent good work, backed by a conspicuous act, may.

It's all in the game. There is no time for reports. You just hear, "C. did good work"; that's all. Every day, it is some one. A man cannot hesitate when he sees to do a thing is certain death; it is his luck, he must do it, and do it on the run. My only fear is I may hesitate a second. I hope not, a thousand times. No one is safe. . . .

. . . K. has made himself understand that the shell you *hear* coming is not yours, because the shell is ahead of the noise. I haven't got this yet, though I have tried hard. This is a good place to find out about yourself, I know that I am not naturally brave; in fact, far from it. But there is one thing I am counting on to help me out: I cannot naturally see any one suffer pain and not go out to give a hand, at least not in this, so I am hoping I shan't make any bad breaks. . . .

Did I tell you I broke the nice pipe; the amber was bound to go out here sooner or later. I found another on "The Ridge" though, so I am not without; and, as I write, laid down in my "Bivvy", I am smoking your Imperial. Another thing! don't send any more socks. It's the limit, the way the Daughters of the Empire of B.C. and other B.C. outfits send socks to this Batt'n. I have a lovely thick snow white pair on right now. We even get clean ones right up in the front line — nearly a pair a day. Our feet are considered very important, and whale oil has to be rubbed in frequently; an officer stands over you while you do it.

Plain chocolate, cakes, anything sweet is what we love. The two parcels I got were perfect. I could kiss you very heartily for 'em.

. . . Dearie, you must know that I am with you and Billie every hour of every day. You are never from my thoughts. I cannot write of it much, not now, but you must know it is there.

12 July, '17.

My dearest Lal, —

The time here is actually beginning to hang heavily. Though there is a whole battalion here made up of the men who have been left "out" for the trip—so many for each—there is nothing to do. We are in a tiny French village which at one time has been heavily shelled; but now never even gets attention from any aeroplane. "Revalley" is at 5.30. At 7.45 we fall in for a parade, and at 8.30 are finished for the day. There are hundreds of little villages and small towns around; but you don't feel like walking places when you haven't a cent. I guess a fellow has an awful nerve to kick while "out", no matter what the conditions; just the same I am getting bored to death. In about a week or so this little place would look like a little heaven. The worst of these kinds of rest, you get thinking—thinking of the waste of time, and the damn foolishness of it all. Just imagine it! here's me, a full private, the lowest pawn in the idiotic game, being played by a bunch of men you will never even see, who play from a position of perfect safety. For this I receive $1.50 a week to spend, the French people being careful to arrange a special scale of prices to relieve you of this magnificent sum *tout suit.* I have just had supper—a piece of bread one inch thick, about four inches square, a piece of cheese one inch square, and a pint of tea. I got this after standing in a line at least half an hour. When—if—I get home, I must begin my life over again from the beginning. If I get killed, the British Government, who is spending more than forty million dollars a day, will most carefully charge you personally for the blanket they bury me in.

If I hadn't come, I would feel too cheap to live.

The only farseeing men have been those who have got themselves commissions in the Army Service Corps and things like that; nothing to do, a private clean your boots, better living conditions than they ever had at home, a certainty of eventually going home — and all the glory. Why in Hell couldn't I have foreseen that ? . . .

I see they have had another air raid over London — serves them damn well right. Could you believe there could be such men living as to have the nerve to stand up and decry reprisals. There are too many of these fat overfed swine all over the world who played Germany's game. The pity is Fritz always seems to bomb the "East End" where the poor people live — ever notice that ? Why doesn't he ever bomb the palaces up "West"? Why? A good many people are wondering about a lot of things, these days. He'll *never* raid that particular part of town. The pawns are the people. But the people are beginning to think. The papers hint it, the men out here say it openly. Air-raid reprisals are of course the only thing to do. If you are having a scrap with a fellow and he punches you in a place you thought he wouldn't, do you merely try to look superior and just carry on with the scrap in your way." I guess not. Is this to be a fight to a finish, or merely an exhibition bout? However—I should worry. They won't bomb Ottawa; and if it doesn't do any other good, it will make the people think harder.

I suppose you read all the ghastly exposure about Mesopotamia. I notice several papers begin to wonder if things may not be something like that over here. Well, of course, I know nothing about the General Staff; but I do know something about the medical conditions, which over in Mesopotamia were so frightful. And no one need worry about conditions as they are on the Western front. After a man once hits the field ambulance, he is alright; if his life can be saved at all, it undoubtedly will be. The attention not only provides necessities, it includes luxuries, and the skill is of the very highest order. I guess that is why every one is tickled when he gets a "soft one." No doubt the Sisters have a lot to do with this. From what I saw at Boulogne, I cannot imagine a more conscientious, hardworking bunch, nor can I see how that particular hospital could be improved in any way. It helps a lot to feel that you will get a fair deal, and everything will be done that can be done, when you are in the line, and Fritz is "handing out Blighties" rather liberally.

I feel all tickled about the medical end of the way my platoon will go into the line this time. It is my idea (and I am in my own mind convinced I have succeeded) to have it equipped to handle any sick and wounded the best of the whole battalion. As I have told you, it is most difficult and discouraging, trying to get supplies from the proper quarter. The suggestion is turned down that we should carry simple medicines in the line — like phenacetin, Cascara and like things. Obviously absurd — as a man goes sick and leaves the trench to go to the Dressing Station, when, if we carried the stuff, he could be treated right there on the spot. I have told you I am on good terms with all of our Company Officers, and I have explained all this and they agree. Again — another thing — the men like to feel that the S.B. is interested in the job and will carry all he can. Well, this trip, when just odd platoons were left out, and the M.O. was away, I made out a compendious list, got the O.C. and Adjutant to O.K. it, and beat it over to a field ambulance of a different division about ten kilometre away. *And* — got the whole works: ointments, spirits of ammonia —(to buck up fellows after being buried, etc.) pills of all sorts and everything. So now I go into the line with as good a kit as any advanced Dressing Station, and we'll be the only platoon having such an outfit. I don't mind the extra weight a bit. I am keen to make good on this thing, and it is all worth it. Also I am tickled about another fellow having joined us from the Taplow Hosp. He was wounded with the Battalion at the Somme last year, and while in Blighty was given a job in the Hosp. and learned a lot. Now he is back in my platoon, and I can call on him in a pinch for help. That makes three of us who can all give help in bad times. Of course the other two — H. and this fellow — carry rifles and are in the line like the rest. I am the only official one for that work. All through the bad times when Fresnoy was lost, I never had any help at all, and many times was at a loss; but now all is different. H. is my assistant, and takes my place if I get hit, and the other fellow is spare man.

So we are all fixed up and everybody is pleased.

Friday, July, the thirteenth.

My lucky day, you remember; but no letter, no parcel, and figs for tea. My luck must have departed elsewhere, or probably it's too hot for it to work. Well the *Saturday* Post was great. After I had read it, I intended writing some more to you, but another distraction came up. Some few hundred yards away is tethered to a traction engine, one of the familiar sausage balloons. Fritz got uneasy about it and actually started shelling it with 6' shrapnel. I guess that doesn't convey much; but ask some one to describe to you the size of 6' shell. On the way over, it makes a noise like two express trains both blowing their sirens. I never saw a balloon shelled like that with such big stuff before. It must be an expensive business and most difficult work. The two observation officers did not phone down to be hauled in, but stayed right with it till dark, when Fritz quit. Imagine shelling a small object like a balloon in the air, from a distance of ten miles away, and with a naval gun. They must be bugs or have something very important to hide, probably the latter. Usually they employ planes to bring these down. It's a great sight to see Fritz swoop down vertically at over one hundred and fifty miles an hour, the balloon burst into smoke and flames, and then notice two white mushrooms slowly coming to the ground (the observers in parachutes), that is, if they are quick enough. The whole business takes about twenty seconds, from Fritz appearing at a terrific height to the conflagration.

We haven't seen any news here for five days. We don't even know what the Russians are doing, or what is happening anywhere! . . .

As I have said before, when you get wounded your troubles don't automatically end — they only just begin. They end when you hit the C.C. Station and a woman gets hold of you.

Kiss little Billie for Dad and tell her to remind poor old forgetful Mummie about her photograph.

Everything here and with me is wonderfully well. I could not be better in health.

15 July, '17. (Sunday)

My dearest Lal: —

One thing I like about the Canuck papers — at least the Vancouver papers, I don't know about the others — they print the officers' and men's names in the lists together. That's just as it should be, of course. In England, some papers don't even print the men's names at all — only officers'. I guess the men don't count over there. All the English periodicals, etc. deal exclusively with officers — the magazine pictures, even the blessed ads, all officers; they make me tired, those people. . . .

Well, as I said last night, we were billeted in evacuated houses. My place was up two fights of stairs, in the attic with two more other fellows. I was just nicely getting to sleep under my overcoat, when the old familiar screech came over, apparently rather close. It was followed by several more. They sound worse at night somehow, and I'm afraid I didn't feel much like sleep. However, I wasn't to have any apparently, as a man came chasing up the stairs looking for stretcher bearers with a flashlight. I had taken all my clothes off, rather foolishly, I guess; but we'd been "bomb proof" so long, I'd almost forgotten about the war. I had to laugh at myself as I hastily got into my boots, forgetting I hadn't got my trousers on, and had to take 'em off and begin all over again. You couldn't light a light, as there were holes in the roof, and then I couldn't find my tin hat. However, I wasn't really very long before I was out in the street and following an Imperial Artillery man to where a man lay who had been hit. I did what I could — it wasn't much — a shell splinter had hit him in the stomach. As we bound it up, he was unconscious and getting cold. The man sleeping under the same blanket with him was untouched. I got four of his bunch to take him away on a stretcher to the advanced dressing station, wherever it was. They seemed to know.

On the way over, I had decided to locate a heap of bricks and mud or something in the street, and spend the rest of the night in the lee of that; but it came on to rain, so I abandoned the idea — I was only about fifty yards from the house — and as Fritz was now shelling another part of the town, I turned in in the attic once more. Again I was just going off to sleep when back came the shells to the old place and F , who was sleeping next me, said, —

"What do you think we'd better do?"

"Get out of here, anyway," I said.

So we came downstairs and went and laid in one of the dugouts I told you of, just in front of the house. I am there now.

17 July, '17.

Last night, we moved from our comfortable chateau to meet the boys in the place where they were coming out to.

It is a large town, the biggest I have seen within the shelling area. Here, there and everywhere in different streets I noticed shell wrecked houses; but, with the town being so large, it isn't as noticeable as in a small village. We were billeted in houses which had been evacuated by civilians, though these are very few. The majority are occupied by women, children and old men. (Since I commenced this page four shells have dropped within about five hundred yards.) Try and imagine, say, Second Avenue — our street is about like that as near as you can compare anything of the old world with the new — the sidewalks gone, the houses dilapidated for want of paint, bits chipped off most of them, the front garden fences all gone and rank grass and weeds choking up everything, most of the windows gone, the whole effect most down at heel and frowsy looking. In front of each house where the sidewalk was, is a hole in the ground, which is a dugout, reinforced with timbers. When a shell comes particularly close, the civilian and military population walking down the street at the time can dive down into these holes, for the moment, then crawl out and continue along until another comes. Needless to say, the women don't wear white shoes and dresses, and "dignity" is forgotten.

After all these months of war, the civilian population have got callous, seem to be able to judge the distance of the shells to a hair, and altogether seem far less interested than the soldiers. The shops and estaminets are all open, and in the Y.M. is a free cuisine nightly. The children walk about unconcerned, selling chocolate and spearmint—and "Ingleech Newspapairs" and never look up unless a shell actually hits in the street. The ground shakes perpetually with our own heavies which are hidden all over the town.

Next day —(or rather evening).

As I told you before, the Division just now is baseball crazy. The thing causes the most intense rivalry—even Generals attend—and the winning team gets a trip to Paris where they will play games against American teams. The rivalry between Batt'ns. in everything, line work and games, is at all times intense; a sneer at a man's Batt'n. is a fight at any time. We kick about our crowd amongst ourselves; but don't let an outsider agree, or it's bad for him.

To lose a piece of trench is like losing a game through being a quitter. It's fine, the spirit; I love it—it's like school and college. I guess this would puzzle Fritz, wouldn't it ? This spirit—

Next day.

Today has been a confounded nuisance; the polishing is getting on every one's nerves. We even have inspection in the afternoons now; it's done to such a limit that entrenching tools have to be cleaned, and both sides of brass buckles, and so on — all for an hour's inspection by some General or other. All the officers seem to be going crazy and harass the fellows to death. We'll soon be glad to get back to the front line, to get away from them; there you only have a lieutenant around. This evening I had a very enjoyable time; the band plays most nights in the "Grande Place" as I see it's called — some name for a small village green! You can sit around on the grass and read and listen to it. The French peasants and miners' wives and children all turn out, and, as it's a quiet little back water of a place far from the high road, no motors or transport going along stirring up the dust. . . .

Thursday.

I think I ought to finish this and mail it.

Long before it reaches you I shall have experienced once again the nerve-racking old *whizz – ker-ump* of Fritz's little shells. I have had a good rest — a peach. Only four men out of a thousand got leave, and I was one. I am sure I never felt better, stronger, brighter, in my life; and my nerves are as good as ever again. In every way, I am far better equipped to face things than I was before the big show in April. I have seen things at their very worst, which is some comfort anyway, and I do not think, from gas to machine guns, old Fritz has anything new for me. "It is written", and all I can do is do all I can for the boys that get hit, and do my darndest not to get napooed myself. Maybe a Blighty will come my way, before the wet weather; then I shall have an opportunity to exercise all my winning ways to obtain a dear little ceasefire job. I have heard it said a man coming back from a trip to Blighty on holiday dreads the life ten times more on his return. Well, I have carefully analyzed my feelings, and I can truthfully say I am less afflicted with "funk" or "cold feet" than I was the first time I set out to go up. In fact — and I am rather surprised myself — I haven't the least bit of funk in me just now. I may have when I get there; but I'm inclined to doubt it. Of course, no amount of understanding or brains will save you from the one which is yours; but a knowledge of shelling at its worst considerably helps you to do instinctively the safest thing unconsciously, in an ordinary strafe.

Another thing I have which is invaluable to me in my particular branch, that is, the confidence of every man and every officer in my outfit in my being on the job when I'm wanted.

I know I have this; I think, too, you will be glad to know it. It is nice to feel that you are trusted and maybe — liked.

The only thing for you to do, too, is to "carry on" and carry on with the biggest and bravest heart you can. You can do this, I know; you had always the better of me in facing hard situations bravely.

We have been told officially there is hard fighting ahead. There is. I know it — you know it. I think we are on the eve of some big things; the place we are going to is going to figure very largely in the news. The Canadians have won a great name. I am not speaking with prejudice. They have all the dash and spirit of the other Colonials ; but — and a big but — they can be relied on not to get excited or go too far; in other words, to obey orders to the letter.

All I have previously said about wanting to get away from it all, of course still goes. I'd give anything to; but I want to go legitimately, if that is the right word.

20 July, '17.

. . . The place I was writing from before got altogether too hot. That same afternoon, a woman got killed, and another shell took the front of a house off; a woman had just gone to a little lean-to shed only a second before, and therefore wasn't hit. Such are the trifles that come between life and death in that town. The amazing thing was that half an hour afterwards the old man, the old woman, and a child were unconcernedly putting old boards up over the shell hole against the weather.

At night, we got orders to move. Eventually we arrived in a little wood and were told to "dismiss." F. and I lay under a tree. Early in the morning, it came on to rain. Next day, we tore down some old buildings, got pieces of rusty, old corrugated iron, and made a sort of lean-to against the tree. It rained all day and the wind was terrific. We covered it with branches broken from the bushes; it helped, but it wasn't rainproof. Life is still very damp, and uncomfy — *very*.

Yesterday K. came back, looking very well and fit, but horribly despondent, as he's missed his leave. I think he intended getting married. Can't now, he says. He'd never try for a staff job down at the base. He asked to come back — would you believe it — because — he wasn't getting his mail. *Some* reason!

You'll see we've had the King over. He was up near us some time ago and reviewed some B.C. Canucks about a mile away. Luckily they didn't call us out. If we had been, I guess we'd have been polishing and cleaning for six months ahead. You should have heard the language of the bunch he *did* see.

Reviews are the biggest bore out here. Apparently those who do the reviewing forget our chief consideration is whether we'll be alive next week, or the one after, and therefore can hardly in the nature of things be wildly enthusiastic in having a brass hat walk by you, who never saw a shell exploded except through a telescope.

I want you to order "The Sunday Pictorial", for *July 15, '17*. In it you will see a picture of the Church Service held on Dominion Day that I told you about. I am about the centre of the bunch of men on this side of it, though of course you cannot see me. I want you to keep it, as it is a fine example of how hot air is dished up to the public. It says: "Enemy Air Craft over a Church Service" — whereas it was our own planes, which of course the photographer knew — so would any of us who used his brain. It's hardly likely about four thousand men would stand packed in a bunch calmly looking up at an enemy aeroplane while the padre carried on with the service. It's like the pictures you see of big bugs in the trenches. Yes — trenches for teaching recruits down at Havre or somewhere. There's always something that gives it away to any one in the know, like showing men with gas masks *not* at the alert — *i.e,* on the chest — or *without* a tin hat.

Now I must finish this. Writing is very difficult. It's wet, cold and windy, and I ain't got no 'ome, at least only a very flimsy one. . . .

27 July, '17.

I feel utterly dispirited to-day. We moved to a different town again, one that's deserted and shelled pretty bad, like the rest around here. Yesterday afternoon I spent with young V. R. and in the evening went up into the front line on a working party. On the way back a shell dropped amongst the bunch and got eighteen. The work, the confusion, all in the dark and everything, was awful for awhile, one boy dying awfully hard with a wound in the stomach — had to be held down for fear of tearing off his dressings. I was called over to see if it had slipped, felt down; but it hadn't, so I went away and they got him off to the station. This morning — as young V didn't come over to see me as usual, I went to hunt him up — to find it was him who had the stomach wound, and he was dead. I went over to the ruined house where the dead were and sure enough it was him, poor kid! He just looked asleep. If only I'd known it was him, when I was called over, I could have given my other cases to other men, and stayed with him till he died. But in the darkness and hurry I never recognized him. The other stretcher bearer that dressed him told me at the time the man couldn't live. I remember I asked him if he knew him; but he said he didn't. And only last Saturday we were going to walk over to the nearby town—H., K. and I to have our photographs taken together; but left it too late. A brighter, cleaner, steadier young boy never came to France. I think he told me he was an only child. I will get his mother's address, and have you write. I cannot. By you get this, I'll have been through—or otherwise—the biggest battle of the war, I guess. If I'm to get it, I shall, I suppose. Well, what is there to say? Nothing. It's my fate alone that can show. Every second of these coming weeks, my heart will be reaching out to you. I love you, dear Lai—am yours—now—and forever. You have been always—are the one perfect thing in my life.

28 July, '17. (Evening)

My darling Lal:—

The weather is lovely, warm, clear, bright blue skies. The nights, though, are getting chilly, and sleeping without covering of any sort is not so pleasant.

It's queer how magnificently confident every one is. I am quite sure it has never occurred to any one that all might not go well; that, for instance, Heinie might put up such a resistance as to stop us. How terrible it must be to be fighting a losing fight; to know you are opposing men who never even figure on your resisting at all, just plan to walk right over you without even contempt, not even with savagery, just in the day's work! Every one knows the artillery will support us to the limit artillery science has gone, as they know the other Batt'ns. are just humans like ourselves, and will go over without hate, without excitement, just because —

It's the job of work we came to do, and we do it. That's all. I have looked to find some difference — some sign in the fellows around that we are going into battle; but there's none, none unless that the mail bag is heavier — if that's a sign. The boys discuss it, of course; but only in a detached way, more as to technical details than anything else. I heard a man wondering if they'd be able to get mail in to us, and kicking because he thought they'd probably be too darned lazy. One fellow did say he hoped there wouldn't be many casualties, but he didn't sound awfully interested. . . .

(I guess) 29 July, '17.

We are on the eve of the most terrific thing in history. Our Batt'n has a most difficult part to play: as each hill is occupied, we will have to take and hold the trench. There will be German trenches which of course will receive very bad shelling. All the time, we shall be carrying supplies up to the firing line — which, in cases like this when an operation is on, is done in broad daylight without cover. The whole operation is going to be terrific, so big, in fact, that some think it will even end the war this year. I'm not saying all this without thinking. I mean it can't make you anxious as, by it reaches you, the operations will be either a success or otherwise, and I'll be either well — or out —

I only wish I could tell you all the details of what I am seeing, and what I know, but that must wait till I'm home. The things happening hourly are so tremendous; the ingenuity, machinery, preparations, all so unbelievably terrific, I couldn't even put it on paper, if I were allowed.

One thing, I'd hate to be in the German front line today — and on. It is my firm belief that it's now or never, the turning point of the war.

There's going to be casualties, and nasty sights, and nerves tried to the limit. I'm nervous — nervous as hell; but I'll make it alright, I'm sure. I mean I won't fall down. The rest — is written —.

A complete victory was snatched from us at the Somme, owing to quite unexpected bad weather. At Vimy, on April 9, it was cloudy, rained, snowed, and utterly prevented a very large advance.

Today it has unexpectedly rained, heavily; aeroplane work at a most critical moment is suspended ; and roads already in very bad shape.

In all probability, the advance will be held up. The trenches, incidentally, will be *hell*. . . .

I am keeping up a good heart—trying not to think of anything nasty—mainly hoping. I'll make a good showing on my job, which I shall try my utmost to do.

Victory will be ours, of course.

My heart and all my soul are yours.

We shall meet again, I know.

30 July, '17.

My dearest Lal:—

The weather has gone clean back on us. Isn't the coincidence amazing—and the bad luck of it! Think, every time we have planned an advance on a huge scale which would of necessity bring the war nearer to an end, the weather has intervened and stopped us. Today it is cold, wet, dirty, not a plane to be seen. The guns go on, though. There are minutes when you cannot hear yourself speak. The "whizz-bangs" don't open up till the zero hour when the boys jump over, or, rather, a few minutes before. Though the ground throbs day and night with this titanic preparation, there are hundreds of hidden guns that have never even fired a round yet. At Vimy, too, there was only a gun barrage; in this are to be all kinds of new-fangled contraptions in addition. I certainly don't envy Fritz. I wonder if the Canadian papers are putting you wise to the thing. The English papers openly speak of it. . . .

As you know, all trenches bear names, like streets. They have to, for map purposes, and so you can find your way about, direct people and everything. What sort of a humorist was the guy who named the trenches we occupy? We enter by "Cork Screw Trench" and through "Suicide Hole ", our resting place being "Murder Alley." He had a genius for the job evidently, and one is not likely to forget the names. . . .

So thorough is this job, that roads have been built in the night right over the shell-torn, open ground, over trenches, and everything, then covered over lightly with soil, so it looks just the same as the surrounding ground. Nothing has been forgotten, you bet!

31 July, '17.

My Dearie Lal: —

Today wet, cold, impossible weather; our bombardment slacking off a bit. Did nothing all day, sat in ground floor room, no ceilings, walls mostly wrecked, no windows, and large opening leading into hall. By tearing beams off outhouse, got wood for fire which we made in remains of the open fireplace. Very cosy when we covered the holes up with waterproof sheets. Heinie quit retaliating altogether.

In afternoon, he had the nerve to send a plane over—circled round just overhead. We could plainly see iron crosses on wings. Fierce attempts were made to get him, one chap having the presence of mind to get his rifle and have a shot. To every one's disgust he got away. We are sore; but I guess the batteries were sorer, as no doubt he got pretty fair photographs. It was a brave act, and you have got to hand it to him. We all expected a deuce of a "strafe" after he got home, but as yet none has come. Slept as usual in the cellar on my stretcher, as none of us had even an overcoat. Haven't slept for nights, owing to the cold.

1 August, '17.

Weather worse—it's damnable. Was there ever such luck! Rain came so badly through roof had to hunt around for corrugated iron to put on the remains of the ceiling beams—that is, on what was once the front bedroom floor. All dry then, huge open wood fire—jake! Noon, heard armies to the North and South had gained objectives, but one had had a hard fight. Do not thoroughly understand it. All seems to be going well, though. Maybe their weather is not like ours.

Evening.

May have to go on working party tonight. Got full supplies of dressings. Got a fine kit now. Was low, owing to busy time the other night. Fritz now starting to come back a bit with overhead shrapnel and 5.9's. One casualty only so far. Mail for every one but me, Cheerful! Got a cold. Dreading trenches; they'll be full of water. Damn the luck! Good weather, which we had every right to count on, and we would have been away ahead — "Gott mit uns."

2 August, '17.

Weather worse and worse, positively awful. Rain incessant — and cold. No news of a move, and no working party last night.

This morning got a very old paper. Young French kids bring papers right up, when they can get hold of them. . . . A French "civile" will face the whole German Army for a franc. They have a Jew or a Scotchman backed right off the map. The papers have the early news of the opening battle in Belgium. We hoped for a complete smash; but what could you do in this weather and without 'planes? Our delayed move was only to be minor, anyway, in comparison with the big show, and now in this weather I don't know what they will do. A success as planned might have ended the war. The Kaiser has some excuse for saying Gott is mit him.

. . . Well — We are not going up. The show is off.

Now's your chance to prove to me that the Almighty is with us. This push was intended, without a shadow of doubt, to finish the war. The weather intervened in favour of the Germans, and the war is prolonged.

4 August, '17.
3rd Anniversary.

Rain of course. That goes without saying. Had a small parade this morning, practicing putting on "Gaspirators." Six seconds is the time allowed and that is ample. I see the morning's paper says the reason there were not more prisoners up north was because our bombardment killed so many—M'yes—quite so!

We have had a small lecture on the Huns' new gas. Large calibre shells of Prussic Acid gas. Gentle creature, the Hun! It has already been christened the "Mustard" shell, as it leaves the ground, where it hits, yellow, and tickles the nose like mustard. It remains effective for as long as thirty hours. You can absorb it through the skin by rubbing your clothes with your hands; in fact, any old way. It seems to be made so you can get gassed with the least possible trouble on your part. "Deadly" is its middle name. A place may be shelled with it, one day, and you go past that place next day, and be gassed. So you see, in spite of everything, the humane German has found another horror to add to the list.

5 August, '17.

Still rain, rain, rain, no change. The trenches and shell holes will now be quite full. Got a paper this a.m., and am not impressed, decidedly not impressed. But we can't fight the elements too, and as Germany has evidently enlisted the weather man on his side, what can we do? It is beyond words. You can safely arrange your Xmas festivities and leave me out.

It's noon, and as yet we have no news of our own wee show. I can't think that we shall stay here much longer. The other battalions in the brigade have done a turn, holding the line till the show opens, and it's up to us.

Eats are poor, awful poor.

Last night, Fritz came back a bit in this little burg. None came too close to our particular bedroom. At least, we didn't consider it too close, though I guess if shells burst near enough to your house in Ottawa to throw mud and bricks down your basement steps, you wouldn't sleep much. It depends on your point of view. Last night was the best night I ever had, with my own pillow and sandbag blanket.

A fellow I know got a nice pocket edition of Service's *Red Cross Rhymes* and lent it me. The Stretcher Bearer one, for which I hoped a lot, I thought rather poor. No one seems ever to have told in writing about the Batt'n. S.B. He is the only Stretcher Bearer that doesn't *stretcher bear*; but goes in, Hves and works with the battahon in the Hne, and does the first aid over the top or behind, all the time. The next nearest are the Fid. Amb. bearers who *bear* only, and go *after* the scrap or strafe, when sent for, to get the wounded out. When not wanted, they are way back in a dugout, the Batt'n S.B. being in the trench or shell hole all the time with the boys. Again, he does not wear a red cross, and, in a counter attack, gets killed along with the rest of the boys, as he is *not classed as a non-combatant*.

. . . He should write one to a trench cooker, the old bully-beef tin with holes. It's just a candle, then a bit of sandbag or shirt flap. How many meals I've cooked on such a range ! By the way, sandbags don't figure much in the war now — only to carry things in. Heinie uses very few. He prefers concrete, and of course we occupy his old lines. The old days of putting France and Belgium in bags is *fini*.

Well I guess it is time to go down into the cellar and try to sleep. I pinched a few sandbags today, tied them together, dried them out, and have what I think will make quite a blanket. Am anxiously looking forward to seeing the paper in the morning. No one has a word of news how the big show in the world is going. Doesn't it seem queer, only a few miles from the battle and you over there have news forty-eight hours in advance. I guess tomorrow will be the last day for us, though there is no change in the weather.

18 August, '17.
Somewhere before Lens.

My very dearest girl, Lal: —

I am anxious to get this out because on Monday at four-twenty we go over the top. It doesn't sound or look much when you write it, does it? But it's — well — a serious undertaking. I want to tell you something first of the big battle. As I write, maybe even you are reading of our big show, a success out and out. What we thought was going to be only a minor affair has turned out to be one of the big things of the war.

Last Tuesday night we came in. Just as we were leaving, it started to pour, and we all thought that once again Heinie's lucky weather man had come to his aid. It cleared up though, and right along the weather has been glorious.

Things had been very quiet all day, but just at the moment that we reached the place where young R. was killed, he opened up with gas and H.E. — a terrific strafe, and we were right in it. It was pitch dark; shells were dropping all round; the din and screech was terrifying. For a second, I was afraid there was going to be a stampede. The fellows got a bit rattled with the gas, and grabbed for helmets. The only thing to do was to rush along through it, as he wasn't shelling beyond the town. I could see clouds of gas coming out of fallen shells, but to get my mask on would have meant dropping my stretcher. I decided to run, and hold my breath. Just then I fell on my head in a new shell hole, stretcher on top. When I'd scrambled out, I was alone. I was scared some, I must admit; but I charged ahead, got there safely, stretcher and all, and joined up, put my mask on for a while, and soon we were out of it, with the shells all bursting behind us. It was touch and go for a minute, and can you believe it — not a man was hit. How I'd have managed if there had been casualties, I dunno' — not in all that gas. Thank God there weren't any!

. . . . At four-twenty a.m. you'd have thought the earth had cracked open. My God, it was marvellous! I don't know how many guns we have, some say one to every three men. Maybe a thousand, maybe ten — I don't know. With the first roar we manned the trench and began to move along to our places some few hundred yards further up the line. No power on earth could keep us from getting on the parapet to have a look. It was too dark to see the men advancing behind the barrage, but the line of fire — ye Gods! Try to imagine a long huge gas main which had been powdered here and there with holes and set fire to. The flame of each shell burst and merged into the flame of the other. It was perfect. It was terrible. The flames were dotted with black specks which were bits of rock and mud. Never has anything been seen like it. And to think on Monday morning I shall advance—me—behind just such a line of fire—into what?

Well, we arrived at our trench and just manned it. No shell came near us; we were quite out of it all. After some while, the barrage died down. Only the scream of the heavies overhead and the whirr of planes and the heavy crump, crumps crump of Fritzie's shells behind us searching for batteries. He might as well have tried to shove the sea back with a broom.

Later, news filtered through from wounded coming back, and engineers, and old men. All the objectives had been taken, all the counter attacks broken, such and such a batt'n had lost heavily, another lightly—and so on. Hill 70 was ours, and the villages and trenches consolidated. Canada had proved herself again. But it is not another Vimy; this is no walk-over, it is a pitched battle. Heinie hasn't quit yet, is hanging on desperately. His air service is better, he comes down and fires on the trenches; but his counter attacks lack spirit, and no wonder. Our guns— my God ! If you could see them—and they say each gun only fired three shots a minute, and they are capable of firing twenty! This isn't war; it's murder. There are as vast numbers of prisoners this time, as at Vimy; but the dead are piled in heaps.

On Sunday night we go to the jumping-off trench, his Hue of Wednesday, and attack. At four-twenty on Monday morning—and that's why I want to write to you (and to Billie).

Luckily I am in the first wave, and taken— that we lie out in the open in advance of the jumping-off trench a ways; and, as we have only five hundreds yard to go, we should be on him before he gets to work on us with his guns. Holding it after we have taken it, will be up to us. Any wounded in the jump-off and in the open I must leave for the second wave, though I guess I'll hate it. In fact, I won't do it, if F. or any one gets it. I suppose I'll be busy most when he puts his barrage on his lost trench. We shall take the trench, that goes without saying. . . .

All the boys are very optimistic—and say, "There's one thing, we are just the very guys that can do it."

Sure we are.

(All the Heinie prisoners I have seen are about eighteen years old, not more, and those who have seen the dead say they are all the same, just kids.)

Our grub is rotten, just when it ought to be good, I should think—only bully and biscuit, no jam or butter, and about a little spoonful of dry tea. I am writing this in an old Heinie dugout— just outside Loos. It's full of rats and, as in all of them, the floor is wet and we have no coats or blanket; but I have salvaged a board to lie on, and, with my rubber sheet, it isn't so bad. Shell proof, anyway. The worst of it is, we have no tobacco or candles.

Well, Lal, old pal, I'll finish this. Whether I see you again or Billie, the next few days will say. I think I'll be able to keep my nerve and do what's right. I hope so. I wonder what you'll be doing, Monday morning. I'll be thinking of you all the time, waiting for the. barrage and the signal.

You'll know all about me, if there's anything to know, by Wednesday or Thursday, I guess. Let's hope it's a hospital bed in Blighty. The main thing is for me to do what is expected of me. Do what *you* would do. Don't let's say anything about anything *really* nasty happening. It isn't going to. I don't feel morbid, or downhearted, or anything; in fact, most hopeful. I hope F. pulls through. I'll be awfully worried about him.

Kiss and love up our little Billie for me — lots and lots and tell her I am thinking of her too — a great deal.

V

A NICE SOFT BLIGHTY

V

A NICE SOFT BLIGHTY

September 1, '17.

Pinned at the head of the sheet is this clipping. (Editor.)

The night falls now, and softly flow
  The red lamps, stretching far;
And rest is here for lads who know
  The blood-red night of war.

Still peace and quiet days at last.
  Grey walls and spreading flowers —
A haven from the raging blast
  Of battle-shattered hours.

Now overhead the hour strikes slow.
  The last birds softly call;
The night falls, and the red lamps glow —
  And God's stars over all.

V.A.D. Hospital,
England.

My very dearest Lal, —

Well, I've got all settled down, though I only came yesterday. To come here after France — the front line of France! It's the limit! But let me tell you.

The house is an English country home. It's lent to the Government as a V.A.D. Hosp. and is used exclusively for Canadians and Australians. I guess it holds about fifty. The staff are all English ladies. Don't look for their pictures in a "sister uniform of costly and studied simplicity" doing "War Work for our soldiers" in a high class English society paper. It won't be there. They are here to help us get well, and apparently make us happy. They succeed completely. Not a man but loves the place. The amazing thing — there are no rules, yet these fellows, fresh from the line, never swear, are intensely polite, go out of their way to help, and generally conduct themselves far better than they ever did in their lives — and like it. Yet the majority of "brass hats" and such like would say it couldn't be done. The presence of just one "military guy" would spoil the working of the whole machine.

It is quite a large house. We sleep in beds, above each of which is a card saying it is kept up by one firm or person in B—— . The only work we do is make this bed. There are several bathrooms, and tons of hot water. The whole place is free to you to run over any time of the day. As I say, there are no rules at all; yet the place is the most orderly, where soldiers have been, that I have ever seen. There are large grounds — I have already played tennis — and lawn golf. You are *asked* not to touch the fruit trees; every tree is loaded with fruit, and is untouched. In France, they put armed guards over fruit trees, and every one, in spite of it, is rifled and most of the branches broken off. In the grounds are open-air sleeping huts for patients needing air. Most of the men here are rest cures; my own case gets no treatment other than fresh air and rest. There is no treatment anyway for gas. There is a billiard room, cards of course, and all games, piano, gramophone, all the latest magazines, etc., and a library, a peach. (I am starting on Ian Hay's books.) In the lovely big rooms are really easy chairs, not the near variety of a Y.M.C.A., and open fireplaces with fires in 'em already. Always there is something doing. Last night a whist drive, tonight a concert. There are also passes for any one to go to B—— any or every day, or to any place you want, from two to seven. I am as happy and contented as I could possibly be. I haven't mentioned the meals. Breakfast bell rings seven-thirty, a *really* breakfast. Dinner is positively scrumptious—two vegetables and meat, and swell dessert, lots and lots of it. Tea four o'clock, and then a meal, a proper meal, at six-thirty or so. And to think! A couple of weeks ago I was a filthy object in the trenches —nervous—verminous—hungry! Sometimes I think I'm going to wake up; it's only a dream.

Tomorrow is Sunday, and I am going to try

and go to church. I see there are services. Do you
know I don't think I've realized all this yet. I'm
quite contented to sit here by the fire and read.
The war is miles and miles away. Now that I'm
civilized again, I must get back to living and
thinking again. I realize what a different me it is
than the one that left Canada. To begin with, I
am horribly irritable, short-tempered, and
nervously self conscious. I don't think alike on
hardly anything I did. I always detested
superficial people; now I *hate* 'em — ten times
worse — I like *really* people ten times more. I
dunno' how you'll like your new husband at all;
he's altogether different. One thing, though: he
likes his wife better than ever he did; he's quite
sure of that. Also he's got an awful longing to see
Miss Billie. She wasn't real in France, he never
thought he'd see her, not really; but now it's
different, and she's most awfully real — and a
thousand possibilities open up.

Sunday Evening.

I had a set at tennis; it's been raining a lot,
and the court wants marking again. I think I'll
do that very special job tomorrow. I've read
all Ian Hay's books. There are so many here
it's hard to choose which to read first, but I've
just decided on one of W. L. Locke's. In the
desk where I am writing, in the French
window of a lovely big room overlooking the

gardens, are albums for fellows to ink stuff in, a sort of memory book. Most of the stuff is weak and rotten, but now and then something good has come along. I must put something on myself, but I don't know what yet. I also came across a list of men's names who had been here, the date they came, and the date discharged. This list was interesting because I see a month here is all that can be safely expected.

3 September, '17.

I have had no mail from any one, from the Battn. or anything. I guess that is because I have moved around so quickly. I still don't know what happened when they went over, that morning. The fellows here from the 29th were casualties in earlier scraps—just minor affairs. I have written F., also K., and another fellow. It is useless writing again; things change so quickly out there, any or all of them may be dead, or in Hospital, or where they can't write. It's rotten not knowing what has happened to F. It is useless to worry, yet I can't help it. He and I were real friends. I only hope he got a nice one. It is the best thing you can wish any one out there—and indeed I cannot see how he could possibly go through the recent stuff and get nothing. I only hope it wasn't a napoo.

5 September, '17.

My dearie Lal: —

I've just come in from one of our strenuous route marches — 45 minutes, it lasts, and consists of a stroll to the nearest Park, a rest, and then a stroll home. Yesterday was a glorious warm autumn day. In the morning, the boy I came in with borrowed from some one he knew here the large sum of ten shillings, five of which he gave to me — and as we are allowed out from ten to twelve, as well as from two to seven, we decided to take the motor 'bus into town. In the afternoon we went with a bunch of Australians to a roller rink — I didn't skate — I don't feel up to it yet, anyway — and later went to the main Y.M. a very large building and had tea — getting in about six in the evening. We played tennis — some of the sisters came to play, and also we had our pictures took on the lawn. Later, supper; salad, bread and butter, and cocoa, a bit of a read at my book, then bed at nine. Can you wonder that when I wake in my little bed, with the nice linen sheets, and get into lovely clean underwear, I feel altogether happy in the thoughts of another ripping day ahead. . . .

If only I could get mail from the Battn.; but there is nothing as yet. Surely, they can't all be Casualties. There are rumours that we have been taken away from Lens. Though we have suffered particular Hell there, I don't suppose a man but will be sore if that happens. We have done all the dirty work, even Vimy was part of it, as he shelled us from there—and it is up to us to take the town; it is our right. Though I guess it's easy for me to talk—here. That's no doubt how the Generals and Brigadiers talk, who do their fighting on the plans from safety. Maybe, if I was up there, I wouldn't care who took the place as long as I was out. It wasn't fighting up there, it was just plain murder. You walked on dead bodies to keep out of the mud.

What a war! We take half a dozen shell holes on the West and lose one hundred miles in the East. Last night there was another air raid. They got clean away, and inflicted heavy casualties, I see. Can you blame Germany for doping it out that she is winning ?

Peace—I think—is further away than it was last year! If America doesn't do something startling next year—and I doubt if she will have had time—I see yet another year of war without peace at the end of it.

                    7 September, '17.
                    V.A.D. Hospital,
                              England.

But K., poor old K. What can we say? Somehow I think K. had a hunch. He was so different from his usual optimistic self; he was so worried not getting his leave; he wanted to get married. But fancy the rotten luck! A fortune in a gold mine in B.C., and a really lovely girl! Now, all gone — for what ?

I remember the last words I spoke to him. We stood, he and F. and I, "on the top." Loos was half a mile behind us — Lens in front. All was desolation; it was evening. We spoke of the coming scrap. K. thought it was going to be easy; but it wasn't the real K. who said it. We stood there quite a time. There was no need to dodge the shells; they were all dropping just behind us. He joked me about my "bunged-up" eyes; it was after I was gassed, and before it had begun to work on me. Poor K.! I'll call on his people, when I go on leave; they are in London. He told me if anything happened to write to his girl. How can I do that? I couldn't. His mother must do it.

10 September, '17.
V.A.D. Hospital,
England.

My dearest Lal: —

I'm all alone practically, and it's a lovely day. There were two "engagements" for this afternoon — a party to go to the pictures, and a tea afterwards. Also a tennis party at some big house near and a "feed." I had my choice,

but couldn't go to either which is most decidedly
rotten luck. Old Fritzie's gas hasn't altogether
left me yet, and decides to come back every now
and then. Last night it bothered me a bit and
again today. I went for a 'bus ride to B. to take a
note to the General Military Hosp. for the
Commandant and have just got back. See! I'm
glad I'm not there still. Just a sight of it, and its
military system, its surly orderly room
sergeants—cease-fire bums who have never seen
France—got my goat at once. How I'll ever
cotton on to things military again, after this
glorious freedom, I dunno', though I guess it will
have to be done.

Tomorrow the big exodus of Canucks takes
place. Believe me they are a sore bunch, and
they have my sympathy. I'd feel just awful if I
was one of them. Out there, it amounts to being
under sentence of death, and it's foolish to
figure it any other way. Again your mental state
is abnormal; you don't think in any way like the
people who live in safety. Every time I have
ever written you, I have been thinking I should
not be able to finish the letter. No wonder it
takes your mental breath away, so to speak,
to turn into a place like this, knowing you
can go to sleep and think of tomorrow. Strange
too how quickly you fall back to your proper
state; already it jars to sit next to a man who
eats with his knife, and reaches in front of

you. Out there, you are just an animal. To even think there's a chance of continuing existence when you can live, and plan, and anticipate, staggers you. Yet—I am thinking there's a chance.

I am still without any news from France—I sent my address to our Battalion Orderly Room and also to B. Co. Clerk. I thought he would forward mail on; but none has come. I wonder what they do with it. If F. had been alright, I feel sure he would have got mail through somehow. F. would take over my job: kit, supplies, etc. I guess I'll know soon now. I wrote asking the Canadian Red Cross to get my mail; it appears they do that for you. I expect some, every mail. We have more than one a day here, but none comes.

I never cease to marvel at my amazing luck. Also to be thankful in a truly humble spirit for it.

Good-bye, Dearie,

Your boy, R. A. L.

L'Envoi

Here is something that goes right to the point, eh?
It's exactly what I am trying to be and do.

A Trench Litany

God of Sabaoth, I but ask
Humbly to bear whate'er befalls —
The dreary, uninviting task,
The sight that sickens and appals.
Ear-rack of never-silent guns,
Burden of bars vicissitude,
Losses of comrades — cherished ones —
To suffer all with fortitude.

If fate vouchsafe me safe return
To firesides of my fond desire,
Grant me the grace never to spurn
The lessons learned in lines of fire —
Chivalry, love, and noble aims,
Knowledge of things undreamed within.
And this — that Private What's-his-Name's
The same as I beneath the skin.

Or if the hollow eyes of Death
Should cast commanding gaze on me.
Bidding me yield the shibboleth
And plumb the black, unfathomed sea —
I pray that I at last may fall
In paths where Honour ever strayed,
And answer the unwished-for Call
 Unquestioning and unafraid.

                    Au revoir
             Your Boy and your Pal,
                            R. A. L.

EPILOGUE

1 N KJ 15 CABLE

SEAFORD Dec 4 1917

EFM

BOARDED LOWEST CATEGORY CANADA GLORIOUS

NEWS KID

147---AM 5th

R.A.L.

'Darby the Yank" fights with the Tanks

A YANKEE IN THE TRENCHES

By CORPORAL R. DERBY HOLMES
OF BOSTON

*Late of the 22d London Battalion of the Queen s Royal West
Surrey Regiment*

12mo. Illustrated. $1.35 net

The actual life of a soldier on the Western front in billets, in the trenches, over the top, across no-man's land and in hand-to-hand conflicts with the Germans is here vividly related by a gallant young American who fought in the English army, until, twice wounded, he was invalided home. Corporal Holmes fought in the battles of the Somme where he witnessed the first of the tanks in action. He participated in thrilling charges and he only ceased "strafing the Hun" when wounded and sent back to "Blighty." He tells his many and varied experiences in trench and billets in a straightforward manner— experiences just like those our United States troops are undergoing in France. This is not a book that depicts mainly the horrors of war, for the lighter side is adequately presented by this soldier boy. It is a narrative to stir the heart and kindle the imagination of the reader.

LITTLE, BROWN & CO., Publishers
34 Beacon Street, Boston